What Did I Do?

A Memoir by

Chuck Jackson

WHAT DID I DO?

Self published – 2017 – by Charles (Chuck) Jackson

ISBN: 13:978-1548327163

Table of Contents

Author's Note

When I wrote this manuscript, my intent was to share a portion of my life story, otherwise a memoir. A memoir by definition needs to be truthful. My story begins at early childhood, more than sixty years ago. Often my memory was fragmented or hazy. Attempting to recall descriptions and conversations from that period of my life unerringly was an impossible task. What I present is my story as best as my memory could recall. The substance of conversations and events have been captured, yet are not intended to be literal.

I also chose to change individual names, some locations, and certain identifying details to protect the anonymity of the people depicted. Whether the experts would accept my presentation as a memoir, might be disputed. Yet, this story is mine to the best of my recollection. The importance is that the reader becomes aware of the essence of my story.

ALSO BY CHUCK JACKSON

ONE MONTH, 20 DAYS, AND A WAKE UP

Acknowledgement

I am still in awe that I wrote this book. My life has been a combination of heartbreaks and joy. Many of my experiences left unhealed scars and some came with hard lessons to learn. Writing my story helped heal some of those scars. Now I am hoping by publishing my manuscript, it will help someone else.

Someone said, if in your life you have one good friend, you've been blessed. I was truly blessed with a true friend with Bernadette Inclan. She heard parts of my story and she was the first friend to encourage me to write it. Anthony Mosca was the second person with whom I shared my life story. Anthony helped with every step of the process and gave me encouragement when I had doubts.

The process of writing this book took over five years and there were numerous people involved. Joy Bayrouty, Bob Bradley, Ted Landry, and my sister-in-law Val and brother Don Nelson read the initial manuscript. Each gave me encouragement to move forward and enhance the writing.

Derrick Miller, Senior Editor with Blue Square Writers' Studio took the project knowing I was a novice writer. Derrick made the process painless and I appreciate all of his advice. His skills made my writing excel.

When Derrick and I were satisfied with the changes, I took one final step. I engaged the help of a good friend, Steve Laskin to do a final proof reading. His keen eye found several overlooked errors. Thank you, Steve.

With each individual involved in putting this manuscript together, I am indebted and cannot thank you enough. Without your help, the publication of this manuscript would not have happened. Consider this your book too.

Introduction

"The worst part of being abused is the betrayal.

The one who should have protected you,

was the one who hurt you."

— Unknown Author

As I grew up, I looked at my world through a dirty window. I would see panes filled with smears of grime and grit. There were areas where the filth was so dense, no light shone through. I hungered and searched for the clear glass of joy and seldom found it. I would see prisms of colored light, yet when I got close, it vanished. The shades of gray light overpowered any hue or luster. *Where were the sunniness and happiness panes? Why did they escape my vision?*

I had no perception of self-esteem or confidence. My craving was to look into a mirror and see a reflection of acceptance. Through the years, I was constantly in pursuit to find approval from someone. When I didn't get it from my parents, I sought it from teachers, relatives, and friends. I was so frantic to find that one person to love me. I would pursue individuals who preyed on my desperation and naiveté. I would walk away hurt and knowing they had exploited me.

My parents told me I was stupid, bad, lazy, and dumb. I would hear it so much, they convinced me they were right. Any attempt to alleviate this perception and gain praise from them failed. The harder I tried, the more confused I became at their response. Often, I succumbed to their canting to escape. Yet, the inner voice told me there was hope. *Don't give up, one day they will see the real you.*

Why was I so different? What could I do to please them? I never understood why I was like a stranger in my own home. *Why was my family different? What did I do?*

I continued to seek inner happiness. Why did it escape me when I would see it all around me? What did I need to do to make it mine? *What made me different? What did I do?*

Today, the veil of secrecy into the inner world of family life is still alive. Child abuse still runs rampant. Why are child abuse and neglect not open to discussion? If you were a survivor of child abuse, could you talk about it? Would it be too horrible to reveal and discuss? How about write about it? There are those who hide due to the stigma attached to its effect. Many have braved the shame, guilt, anger, and depression to tell their story.

I challenge you to read my account as one of those survivors. I want to immerse you into my dark world where I was invisible. It was from a period where family and friends looked away rather than get involved.

I want you to follow the years when they told me I was irredeemable, and I tried to prove them wrong. I attempted to perfect myself to please others. I pursued a warm touch or a word of praise. I longed for love.

Please join while I share my story, which kept me from personal growth and happiness. Follow my story where I broke the barriers to bring purpose, validity, and contentment to my life. Will you follow my story and answer the evasive question — What did I do?

"For those that understand, no explanation is needed.

For those that do not understand, no explanation is possible."

— Unknown author

Chapter 1 – The Beginning

"The greater a child's terror and the earlier it is experienced,
the harder it becomes to develop a strong and healthy sense of self."
Nathaniel Branden – *Six Pillars of Self Esteem*

My life as an infant started with abandonment. In the first months, my birth mother would visit me on weekends at the orphanage where she had left me. When she became pregnant with my brother, she returned to her childhood home in Kansas. Knowing she had no resources to raise her children, she gave her two illegitimate boys to separate families.

Research tells us of the long-term effects of abandonment and neglect is fear and low self-confidence. Infants' natural instinct is to seek comfort and security. When it is withheld or unavailable, they excessively cry. Extended periods of neglect cause the individual anxiety and behavioral problems. When my parents adopted me, I came with some dysfunctions. I am sure those first months were difficult for them.

From my earliest memories, I was told I was adopted. Mother would tell me how they found me abandoned and in need of a loving family. She told me my dad wanted a son who would make him proud. "Look at all we do for you. We do this because we love you." She concluded her speech by saying, "So why can't you behave?" I would promise her I would try harder.

I was a towhead and overly sensitive. I remember wanting my dad's praise and never receiving it. I lived in fear of my dad's severe discipline. *Why can't I please him? Why do I feel different? What did I do?*

Because of fear and anxiety, I compensated by smiling. I learned with a smile, I could get attention. A smile would create a distraction to avoid the emotional pain.

* * *

The family of my adopted dad, William (Bill) Johnson, owned a farm in northern Minnesota. He was the oldest and the only boy of his three siblings. It was rare Dad talked about his family, but when he did, he portrayed his father as quite stern. He said the family rarely showed one another affection. He was 5'7", quite muscular, with beautiful jet-black hair and piercing blue eyes. It was unusual for rural boys to complete high school when Dad was young. Yet, his parents made the sacrifices so he did. When World War II broke out, he joined the military (Army Air Corps; later to be the Air Force). After basic training, he went to San Angelo, Texas where he met my mother. Dad was a perfectionist at home as well as in the military.

June Montgomery (my adoptive mother) was born in West Texas. She was the oldest and had two brothers and two sisters. During her youth, her father worked in a cotton gin factory and her mother worked as domestic help. When she talked about her childhood, she stated she resented having to stay home after school. With her mother away from the home, she had to care and cook for her siblings. After high school, Mother moved to San Angelo. She completed nursing school and graduated as a registered nurse (RN). While working at a local hospital, she met my dad when he was recuperating from an appendectomy. Her picture portrays a petite woman, 5'4", dark brown hair and eyes, and a beautiful smile. My parents married in 1940.

In 1942, Patricia (Pat), my sister and the only natural child of my parents, was born. She resembled Mother with her dark brown hair and eyes. When my sister was young, she was a typical tomboy to the pleasure of my dad. Yet, it irritated my mother when Pat was not feminine or had no interest in domestic activity. Where I failed at sports, Pat excelled. Dad would shame me by asking how I could let a girl beat me.

In 1947 at the age of fourteen months, my parents adopted me. Dad was stationed at Smokey Hill Air Force Base outside of Salina, Kansas.

In 1949, Dad transferred to Goodfellow Air Force Base near Abilene, Texas. These are the earliest years of my memory, and while we lived in Abilene, I completed first and second grades.

I was not the rough and tough boy my dad wanted. He was always calling me a "sissy," "crybaby," and "little girl." When I allowed other boys to bully me, it would anger Dad, and he would spank me. Dad had a wide leather belt he kept in the top of his chest of drawers. To emphasize the discipline, he would have me go and retrieve the belt. I would have to lie over a chair or the side of the bed. He would double the belt before the spanking. He would not have me lower my pants; yet, I had welts on my butt and upper thighs.

Growing up, I feared my dad. Yet, I was determined to gain his praise. I would feel embarrassed that I did not meet his approval as a son.

As with Dad, I spent much of my life trying to please my mother too. She was strict, manipulative, and devious. I avoided seeking her comfort. If I went to her for comfort, she viewed it as a weakness. I did not understand when she would admonish Dad when he lost his patience with me. She would later scold me for making my dad angry. Discipline from mother came in the form of guilt or humiliation.

* * *

One of my early memories was an incident that began as innocent child's play. The neighbor girl, Susan, and I were playing Tarzan and Jane behind her house. We removed our clothes thinking it would be more authentic. When Mother caught us, her face turned red and her eyes narrowed. "What are you doing? Where are your clothes?" I blushed, as my head lowered. "Kenny—Where are your clothes?" I feared looking at her and pointed over by the bushes where both Susan and my clothes lay.

"You get your clothes and go to your room." Mother found a stick. As I grabbed my clothes and headed for the house, she was right behind me swatting me with the stick. She left me in my room and told me to not get dressed. While I waited, she took Susan home and told her mother of our escapade.

When Mother returned, she brought a small standing mirror and positioned it so I could see myself naked. "You like being naked, you can stand there and look at yourself. Did you tell Susan to take her clothes off?

I stood in front of her, head down, my hands covering my genitals. "No ma'am. Susan took off her clothes first," I whispered.

As I stood in front of the mirror, Mother brought in Susan's mother, my sister, and finally my dad to witness my nakedness. Each time she scolded, "Look at Kenny. He is a nasty little boy. If he thinks it is so much fun being naked, he can stay that way."

This incident stayed with me for years. Any time I had to remove my clothes with anyone around, I would feel embarrassed and dirty. My male cousins and friends would strip down to change for swimming, gym, or a bath and it didn't seem to bother them. I was always uncomfortable.

* * *

I do not remember at what age I was, but I had a stuffed dog I cherished. In fact, I couldn't sleep without him. If we traveled away from home, he had to come with me. I don't remember his name, so we will call him Buster. Even when my dad made fun of me, Buster remained my security. When my world turned upside down, I would cuddle with Buster. He often had a wet face from my tears.

Buster was creamy colored with brown spots and had long floppy ears. His eyes expressed sadness and they reminded me of a Basset Hound. His body was made from flannel and in the early years, his stuffing was sawdust. He would squeak when you squeezed his front right paw. Even as a teenager, Buster laid on my bed.

14

I remember after receiving a spanking from my dad, I would cuddle, cry, and whisper to Buster. I would tell him what I thought I did wrong and he would tell me to try harder to be a good boy. Too many times, Buster was the only love I felt.

By the time I was nine or ten, Buster started having an odor. Mother complained, "You need to throw your old stuffed dog away. He is stinking up your room." I would tell her I couldn't just throw Buster away. I tried to wash him. After a couple washings, the bag containing the sawdust broke open. Buster started leaking liquid sawdust. My heart was breaking because I believed Mother would now make me throw him away. I put him out in the sun to dry.

On the second day when I came home from school, Buster was sitting on my bed and he looked new. He was fuller and softer than before. He still had signs of wear, but he sat taller than before. Although Mother denied it, she had taken Buster and replaced his stuffing with a cotton batting. She renewed Buster's life and he gave me several more years of comfort.

* * *

In 1954, my dad received orders to go to Japan. When he left, my mother took my sister and me to live with my grandparents. Grandma and Granddad lived in a small house in Mesquite, a community near Dallas, TX.

Granddad was not a big man. In fact, he was 5'6", 160 pounds, had thinning gray hair, splotchy complexion, and spoke with a soft West Texas accent. He injured his right leg in a work related accident and he walked with a limp. His attire for work and around the house was a pair of denim overalls, the ones with large metal buttons that hooked the shoulder straps to the front.

Granddad was reserved, sociable; yet, you would find him off by himself at family gatherings. I don't ever remember hearing him say

15

anything demeaning; he always looked for the good in everyone. Granddad loved his family, but Grandma was the matriarch.

Granddad did not drive a car. Most days, I would go with Grandma to pick him up from work. I would watch for him as he exited his workplace. When I spotted him, I would run to meet him. He always carried a black lunch box and he would let me carry it back to the car. I would open the lunch box, knowing he always left a cookie or a piece of candy. He would smile and tell me I could have it.

The year we with lived with my grandparents, Granddad was the center of my life. He gave me the attention and love I craved. He allowed me to follow him everywhere like a puppy. When confused or upset, Granddad would pull me close, and talk softly to me.

Behind Grandma and Granddad's house was a vacant lot that they owned. Granddad utilized the property for a garden. He raised several types of vegetables, melons, and his pride, sweet onions. I would spend hours with Granddad while we weeded, watered, and harvested his garden. While together, he would tell me stories of when he was a little boy or when my mother was growing up. His stories usually had a moral or a humorist inference.

Mesquite did have a Safeway grocery store. Yet, Grandma preferred using the small grocery store owned by a man from their church. The store had wooden floors, worn uneven, and they squeaked as you walked the aisles. The store carried everything from fresh fruits and vegetables, meats, canned goods, to toiletries. Even with the limited selection, my grandparents preferred shopping there.

Granddad and I would watch television together and we had our favorite shows. Granddad loved the old movies, especially those with Ma and Pa Kettle, Laurel and Hardy, and Amos and Andy. He also enjoyed the John Wayne Westerns. When we got ready to watch TV, he would sit in his large rocker and I would crawl up in his lap. He would tickle me and then tease me about sitting still. One of my favorites shows was *Francis the*

Talking Mule. Granddad would imitate the voice of Francis, and it would make me giggle. I would make him repeat it and he always did.

Grandma would send Granddad to the store for whatever she needed for preparing dinner, and I would walk with him. These were my most memorable times with Granddad. He would hold my hand as we walked and I would tell him about my day at school. When finished, he would tell me how proud he was of me. He often teased me about the neighbor girl in my class. I would blush and it would make him chuckle. I was in heaven for the love I would feel from him.

***

For Halloween, the year I went to the Mesquite School, they had a party and costume contest. A neighbor girl was in my class and our mothers made our costumes. I don't know if the girl was aware of our costumes, but I wasn't until two days before the party. We were to be Raggedy Anne and Andy. Our mothers had worked hard to make the costumes authentic. The costumes were exacting for the characters' looks and dress. The only problem, I wasn't going as Andy.

When Mother showed me my costume, I cringed. "I can't wear that. Everyone will make fun of me."

Mother said, "It's a costume. Don't be silly. It will be fun."

"But Mother—"

"Don't Mother me—you are going to wear it. What do you care what people say, everyone knows you are a sissy."

No amount of my pleading was going to change her mind. I went to Granddad to argue my case. When he spoke to Mother, she said, "I spent a lot of time and money on their costumes. I don't want to hear any more about it. He will wear it."

The day of the party, Mother brought the costumes and makeup. When I changed in the boy's bathroom, the teasing began. I went speechless while I blushed with embarrassment. I couldn't believe my mother was making me dress as a girl.

With our makeup completed, Raggedy Anne and Andy joined the party. Not only did we win our class best costume contest, we won the school-wide contest. Even though we won, I was still embarrassed. Halloween night, Raggedy Anne and Andy were a great hit in our neighborhood as we went trick-or-treating. Although my bag was brimming with candy, I couldn't wait to get home and take off the dress, red wig, and makeup.

* * *

Who knows what made Mother decide, but she finally consented to Dad's appeals for us to join him in Japan. In March of 1954, we left from San Francisco, by a military transport ship, to Japan. I celebrated my eighth birthday onboard the ship. We also celebrated Easter. We joined numerous other dependents on the stern of the ship for a sunrise service. The sky was filled with shades of pink, azure contrasting with the indigo of the ocean. There was a beam of bright sunlight illuminating through the clouds. I was convinced I was visualizing God's light shining on our ship.

The day we reunited with my dad, I was so excited I ran and jumped into his arms. He instantly pushed me back on my feet. "Quit acting like a sissy. Everyone is looking at us."

I didn't understand what I had done wrong. When I looked around, I noticed people smiling at us. I stepped back while my sister and Mother hugged him and received a kiss.

While in Japan, Dad insisted I learn to swim and play Little League baseball. I became a proficient swimmer, but I struggled in playing baseball. When our baseball season started, most games I sat on the bench. I practiced hard with a neighbor boy and teammate. By the end of the summer, I was starting at third base. I wanted my dad to come to my baseball games, yet when he did, I regretted it. The games he did attend, he ridiculed and made fun of any errors I made. He scoffed, "You play like a girl."

While in Japan, nothing my dad could do made Mother happy. She would throw a tantrum and yell at him. "Bill, I can't believe you would drag your family over to this God forsaken country." He would roll his eyes and turn red with anger. These arguments became frequent, and when they erupted, my sister and I would retreat to our rooms. Being isolated in my room gave me security, yet the loneliness was overpowering.

While in Japan, Mother's domestic life was easy. They required military families to hire the locals for domestic help in our home. Our maid was a young woman in her late teens, who did everything around the house. For holidays and special occasions, Mother would cook those meals. Even with the easy life, Mother was complaining. I would try my best to avoid any interaction with her. Yet, I remember she sent me to my room, often without dinner.

* * *

As I grew up, there were two sides of my mother. Her normal self was impatient, stern, and strict when it came to my behavior. She never hesitated to tell my dad when she was feeling the reprimand from her wasn't enough. When she did, it would result in a spanking. Going to her for comfort, a hug, or support was always rejected. "Don't come crying to me. If you had done as you were told, you wouldn't be in trouble." She stated mothers who babied their children were making them weak. "You don't make it in this world by complaining. Get tough and don't let anyone walk on you." Yet, she participated in my treading.

Those times when she applied the guilt, her lower lip would quiver and the big alligator tears would well up. "You know we love you and we only want what is best for you. After all we have done for you, this is how you treat your mother? You should be ashamed." She succeeded in her objective and I would leave feeling guilty. I would ask myself, *what did I do?*

The other side of Mother was the result of her natural aptitude for nursing. Dad required her to stay home to raise her two children plus maintain our home. She never kept it a secret that she resented it. When I finally started high school, Dad relented and allowed her to return to nursing.

As a child, I was often sick. My resistance to childhood viruses, colds, etc. was low. When exposed, I would get sick. I would run a fever and she would confine me to bed. Several times the fever was so high I would hallucinate. Mother would immerse me in ice baths to battle the fever. Colds always turned into bronchitis. Mother would place me under steam tents to prevent pneumonia.

Each time I was sick, Mother flipped her psychic switch and became the loving, comforting mother and caretaker. She was attentive, compassionate, and thorough with her care. I often wonder how many times I would have been critically ill if it hadn't been for my mother's nursing skills.

These were times when she would hold me and give me loving attention. It was emotive to have her comfort. Yet, you had to be sick to be the recipient of this attention. As soon as she determined you had recovered, the switch turned. "You can get out of bed now. Quit acting like a baby, you're not sick anymore."

* * *

After being in Japan for eighteen months, we returned to Seattle for Dad to reenlist. I don't think there was ever a question Dad would not reenlist. Mother attempted to convince Dad to go to Texas so she could be close to her family. With the reenlistment completed, we headed east for reunions with the families.

The first leg of our trip was to Park Rapids, Minnesota where Dad's family lived. Before we left Park Rapids, there was a family reunion. I met more aunts, uncles, and cousins than I could count including my great grandparents. After a two-week stay, we headed south for Texas.

When we arrived at Grandma and Granddad's house, Mother's family was waiting. Reunited with her family, Mother was in tears and swore she would never go overseas again.

It elated me to be back with Granddad. To me, he had aged while I was gone. Granddad still had his garden and we spent some quiet time working in the garden. As was our routine before, we would walk hand-in-hand to the store. He chuckled and asked, "Did you miss your old granddad? I bet you were having so much fun, you didn't even think of me."

I knew he was teasing, yet I felt myself blush. "Ah, Granddad; you know I missed you. I couldn't wait to get here." He squeezed my hand as we continued to walk.

Dad's new base assignment was Sioux City Air Force Base in Sioux City, Iowa. Mother was not happy with the assignment. No location would have made her happy except somewhere near Dallas.

When our visit ended, it was harder this time to leave Granddad. I wanted to stay and go to the Mesquite School. As we loaded the car, I noticed Granddad off to the side. His shoulders drooped and his eyes were red. When I went over to him, he pulled me into his arms in a loving hug.

My voice broke, "Goodbye Granddad — I love you."

I could feel his tears splashing onto my face. "You be a good boy and mind your parents. Granddad loves you too." He reached for his handkerchief, wiped his face, and walked back to the house.

I am convinced that even back then, he was aware of the abuse.

Chapter 2 – The Iowa Years

"Over and Over
I tried
And Over and Over
You Lied
And Over and Over
I Cried
And I Don't Know Why"

Posted by: Say-No-To-Child Abuse
September 7, 2012

The interaction of our family changed in the first years we lived in Iowa. Mother was always domineering and this did not vary, it just got stronger. Dad seemed frustrated by her dominance and his anger was often uncontrollable. As his anger intensified, I became his target for release. The spankings turned to whippings and included slaps, kicks, and punches. The verbal attacks paralleled the physical in frequency. Mother saw his deplorable behavior, yet did nothing to protect me. Instead, she harassed him for his outbursts. In turn, it amplified his frustration and fury, which only left me battered and confused. There were times I went to school or church bruised, but no one interceded.

After the first incident where I had visible trauma, Dad threatened me. "You had better not tell anyone about how you got those bruises. It's nobody's business about what goes on with our family. If you know what's good for you, you will keep your mouth shut. Do you understand me?"

Seeing the intensity on his face, I felt my body stiffen. "Yes, sir," I whispered. As he left me sitting in my bedroom, I began to wonder, *If someone did know, what would they do? Would Dad get in trouble? Would he hurt me more?* All during the night, I kept waking up with nightmares.

When the second or third incident of visible bruising happened, my gym teacher noticed the bruises. When I came out of the shower, he asked, "How did you get those bruises on your back and butt?"

I heard my Dad's voice echo in my head. "I slipped on the stairs going down to our basement," I lied. The coach gave me a look, which told me he knew I was lying. I looked away, and finished getting dressed.

My best friend at the time was the neighbor boy. He knew what was going on. He had seen my dad's anger and the abuse. I begged him not to tell anyone the truth.

I don't remember when this happened, but I do remember the incident. It was typical of the swiftness and viciousness of Dad's anger. When we had dinner, my normal place to sit was adjacent to Dad's position at the head of the table. We had a typical chrome kitchenette table and chairs from the 1950s.

Mother was serving potatoes and gravy that evening. I had finished putting gravy over my mashed potatoes when Dad barked, "There are other people at this table who might want some of the gravy. You don't need that much."

As I started to answer, I got a backhand across my face hard enough to knock me out of my chair. When I fell, my arm caught my plate, sending it off the table and hitting the wall and floor. The shattered plate and food was scattered on the floor and some stuck to the wall.

Not moving from his chair, he berated me: "Don't you back talk me!"

As I sat on the floor attempting to figure out what had happened, the family continued eating. After a couple minutes, Mother said, "Well — are you going to just sit there or are you going to clean up your mess?"

I gathered the broken plate and food and placed it in the garbage can. I then got a wet sponge and cleaned the remainder of the food off the floor and wall.

Before I finished, Dad said, "Since you have such a smart mouth, when you get done, go to your room and think about what you did."

I spent the remainder of the evening in my room still confused as to what I had done wrong.

* * *

In my private moments, I tried to understand what I had done so wrong. Friends at school had gotten into trouble and their parents did not treat them this way. *Why did mine? What did I do?*

I would fantasize another family would come rescue me. They would call the police and my dad would get into trouble. They would take me away and they would love me.

During this period, I spent many hours confined to my room. It was a lonely and confusing time. I kept thinking my parents didn't want me, let alone love me. *What did I do?*

What is pathetic was that I would go right back attempting to please my dad to get his praise. As hard as I tried, he always found something wrong with my assigned chores. When he did, the cycle replayed itself. I didn't understand, yet I kept trying. My attempts were never successful.

* * *

Upon our arrival at Sioux City Air Force Base, we had difficulty locating a house. We searched for three days before finding a farmhouse to rent. It was twenty miles from the base and outside the small community of Lawton. Mother was furious when she found out about the housing issue.

"Now Bill," she admonished, "where do you expect your family to live? I'm not living in some dump with mice and roaches." The argument escalated when the farmhouse included an infestation of roaches, mice, and rats.

I enrolled in fourth grade and there were twelve in my class. My sister started her first year of high school with a class of seven. From the very first day, they welcomed Pat and me into the school.

I found I had an interest in music and began playing the trumpet along with other brass instruments. After playing for a year with a used trumpet provided by the school, my mother purchased a new one for me. However, I was not to tell my dad and I was to pay her back. I didn't have any money, other than the measly allowance they gave me and often withheld. She always reminded me that I owed her the money.

I never received my parents' praise for my musical talent. It was obvious Dad would have preferred I spent my time playing sports. Mother never hounded me to practice; in fact it was the opposite. She would yell, "How much longer do I have to listen to that racket? Don't forget you have chores to do before your dad get's home. Do you have your homework done?" Even without their encouragement, by the time I was in sixth grade, I was playing with the high school band. Yet, they rarely attended our concerts.

It was after two months of living in "the dump" a house became available within the town of Lawton. The conditions of this house exceeded the previous one and we moved in. Mother seemed content with the new house since it was clean, warm, accommodating. It was close enough for my sister and me to walk to school.

* * *

During the years we lived in Iowa, the verbal and physical discipline escalated. I don't recall having difficulty outside the home, yet I felt there was turmoil. My parents' displeasure with me seemed insurmountable and the punishments became more severe. Frequently they restricted me from attending school activities. I couldn't go out and play with my friends. I was sometimes forbidden from playing my trumpet.

I would sit in my room staring at the wall. Buster and I would cuddle. I couldn't concentrate on my homework. I started failing tests at school and my grades declined. When that happened, the punishment intensified. I felt there was nothing I could do that would make my parents happy. My fantasies of being rescued by another family returned, as did the fretful sleep and the nightmares.

When I was in the sixth grade, my parents thought my behavior was out of control. Dad told me I was beyond redemption. Mother accused me of being ungrateful for all they did for me.

When confronted, I kept asking myself, *What did I do wrong? Why are they so mad at me?* I was too scared to look at Dad. I knew if I started crying, he would say, "Stop blubbering or I'll give you something to cry about."

Mother would add, "If you would do as you were told, you wouldn't be in all this trouble."

I would ask myself, *What do I have to do to please them? I try my best, but nothing I do is right. They hate me – I know they don't love me.*

* * *

Several weeks later, on a Saturday morning, Mother woke me early and sat on the edge of my bed with a stern look on her face. I knew something was wrong. She announced, "Your Dad and I have decided we are sending you to Boys Town. Maybe they can do something with you. Go get your suitcase and I'll help you pack your clothes."

"What? Why?" I cried. I wasn't sure I had heard her right. "This can't be right – sending me to Boys Town?" I felt my body tense and begin to shake.

"Don't ask questions. You know why. If you had done as you were told, we wouldn't have to be doing this. Now get up and get the suitcase." Although I pleaded and promised I would do better, it was to no avail. She helped me pack, all the time telling me this was my fault.

Boys Town was in Omaha, Nebraska, approximately 100 miles south of our home in Iowa. Boys Town was a combination of orphanage, juvenile detention, and home for rebellious boys.

When it came time to leave and we headed for the car, Dad said, "Get in the back so I don't have to look at you." I remember staring into space and asking myself, *Why are they doing this?* I tried to remember what I had done that was so horrible. It didn't make sense. *They are taking me to*

Boys Town and dumping me like I'm garbage. I know they don't love me. This proves it.

As we got closer to Omaha, I began telling myself this was a good thing. *Since they don't love me, I'm better off at Boys Town. I won't have to listen to them yelling at me all the time. I won't be beat. I don't care anymore – they can go to hell.*

Dad barely spoke, making the trip seem even longer. I remember him saying, "You only have yourself to blame. We warned you. Now you'll have to deal with the consequences."

Once we arrived, I waited in the lobby of an administrative building while Dad met with a priest. When Dad came out, he walked past me, saying nothing. He went out the door and drove off. My heart sank; there was no denying my parents had actually dumped me. I began crying. I could never remember anything hurting this much. I was loudly sobbing and moaning. My breathing became short and then it turned to hiccups. I couldn't stop the sobbing.

The receptionist came over with a box of tissues and tried to console me. I finally quieted down. It didn't seem real, that Dad would leave without even saying goodbye.

Who cares, I told myself. *They don't want me anymore. I'll be happier here.* Yet, I kept looking out the window expecting to see my dad's car return.

I waited for what seemed like hours before the same priest requested I follow him to his office. As we sat at his desk, he asked me, "Do you know why you are here?"

I had my head lowered and didn't look up when I responded. "My parents don't want me anymore."

"No — your parents want us to teach you how to be obedient and respectful."

The tears started again. "I try my best to be a good boy. I don't know what I am supposed to do; they always seem to be mad at me." He concluded by telling me if I had shown respect to my parents and did as I was told, I would not be here. He then sent me out to the lobby and told me someone would be coming to take me to my dorm.

I sat for the rest of the afternoon and stared out the window. Anytime I saw a car, I would look to see if was Dad's. Then I would get angry with myself for wanting him to come back. I kept telling myself I was better off here.

After the receptionist had left for the day, the same priest came and sat down next to me. He told me he had received a phone call and my parents wanted to give me a second chance. Again, he lectured me about being obedient and respectful. Then with a prayer and a blessing, he sent me outside to wait on my dad and he locked the door as I exited.

It was dark and the only lights were the two sconces on either side of the door. The parking lot was empty and I kept looking for Dad's car to come. With the sun down, the temperature was falling and there was a brisk breeze. I zipped my jacket, raised the collar, and put my hands in my pockets to try to stay warm. I watched every car come down the street and my heart would drop when I realized it was not Dad's car.

After over an hour, I spotted his car as he turned into the parking lot. My heart was pounding and even though I was cold, my upper lip was sweating. I didn't want to look at him; I knew those piercing eyes would look right through me.

As I put my suitcase in the trunk, he said, "This wasn't my idea. This upset your mother and she asked me to bring you home. She wants to give you another chance. If it was up to me, I would have left your ass here." I knew better than to say anything. He continued his rant, yet I wasn't listening. We were going home, yet I didn't feel relieved. All I could think about was Dad's anger. *Would he beat me again once we got home?*

When we arrived home, most of the lights were out. Dad told me to go straight to bed. From my bedroom, I could hear my parents argue. I heard Mother ask, "Didn't you tell them how much trouble he was causing us?"

"I did. They told me we had to pay the cost of boarding him. If we didn't want to pay them, then we had to sign custody over to them."

"That's stupid, all that money spent to teach him a lesson. If you weren't going to pay them, why did you leave him?"

"It was your damn idea to send him there. I would have sent him to Hank's. He told me he would keep him so busy he wouldn't have time to get into trouble. Now do you have any other brilliant ideas?"

"Shut up—if you didn't treat him like a dog, he would be more respectful to me. Just because your dad beat you doesn't mean the same thing will work with him. Now what are you going to do?"

The argument continued with each blaming the other for the failure of their plan. It was clear that they didn't want me. They were still shouting at each other, but I wasn't listening. I still couldn't figure out what I had done. I lay in bed staring at the ceiling. The last thing I remembered, Mother was crying and Dad said, "I've had all the shit I can stand. You figure out what you are going to do. I've had enough. I'm going to bed."

The next morning, my sister woke me announcing breakfast was ready. I put on my robe and slippers and went downstairs to the kitchen. Mother gave me a warm greeting and told me to go get washed up. Dad sat reading the paper and said nothing.

After breakfast, we got ready and attended church. When we came home, the rest of the day was like any other Sunday. Dad sat watching some type of sports on TV, while Mother prepared Sunday dinner. Pat was out with her friends. I went out and played with the neighborhood boys. Not once that day or any other time thereafter did my parents ever mention that horrible Saturday. It was if it never happened.

For months afterwards, I could not get over the fact my parents did not want me. I was miserable and could not find a way to shake the rejection. Not thinking it would get back to my parents, I asked Pat if she knew why they sent me to Boys Town. She replied, "What? What are you talking about?" She knew nothing about it and accused me of making it up. A week later, my dad warned me about keeping family matters to myself.

Again, I wondered, *What did I do?*

* * *

The summer after I turned twelve, Dad drove me to his oldest sister and brother-in-law's farm located in northwestern Minnesota (Warren). I was to work alongside their three boys. Uncle Hank and Aunt Ruth's farm was large. It took not only the whole family, but also extra help over the summer to handle all the required work. Even though it was hard work, I found it enjoyable working the summer on the farm.

Uncle Hank was of German heritage. He was big built, over 6 feet, and 230 pounds of solid muscle. He had sandy hair and penetrating blue gray eyes. As intimidating as he looked, he was the opposite. He was a big teddy bear, who loved his family and worked hard to provide a good life for his family.

Aunt Ruth was petite, yet she looked similar to her older brother (Dad). Like her husband, her appearance could be intimidating. She was intense, a perfectionist and took no guff from her husband and three boys. She was a caring and loving mother, yet she did not tolerate any horseplay in the house. She was a superior cook and I loved her homemade bread.

I spent many days alone driving a tractor. I was preparing fields for winter wheat or tilling the potato furrows for weed control. It gave me the opportunity to think about my home life. When I thought of the conflicts with my parents, I would feel my body tense and the sweat would intensify. To avoid the anxiety, I would escape into my world of fantasy. In those daydreams, I was living on the farm and going to school with my cousins.

The times my cousins, Uncle Hank, and I worked together were happy times. It didn't matter if we were baling hay, stacking it in the barn, or milking cows. We had fun. There was always a lot of teasing, pranks, and always some horseplay. Everyone worked together to get the chores done. Uncle Hank enjoyed initiating competition between us boys. The loser had to do some chore everyone hated, like scooping manure. Several times, Uncle Hank took us fishing on Saturday nights.

I pleased Uncle Hank with my work and he told me if I wanted to return the following summer, I had a job. I wanted to ask Uncle Hank if I could live with them. Towards the end of the summer, I rehearsed my speech to convince them. However, I couldn't come up with a justification without telling Uncle Hank why I wanted to leave home. I knew there would be trouble if Dad found out. Consequently, I never asked. When summer ended, I dreaded having to return home.

When I returned home, Mother had bought me some new clothes for school. They looked so juvenile to me. I could not believe she expected me to wear them. I didn't say anything, but my expression must have given me away. Mother said, "If what I pick out is not good enough for you, then buy your own." I did.

Beginning with that summer, until I left home, my parents stopped giving me any type of allowance. In fact, other than providing food and shelter, I paid for my personal expenses. With my paper route and summer jobs, I always had money. I purchased all my school clothes, haircuts, entertainment, and other personal spending. In addition, I saved enough to have a small college fund for myself.

* * *

Before I started first grade, doctors found I had amblyopia (lazy eye). There was no treatment then. In fact, even today, the treatment is limited unless caught before a child's eye develops. This condition limited my vision, and was responsible for poor sports ability. With amblyopia, when using only one eye, the individual has depth perception difficulty. To this day, I have to compensate for my poor depth perception.

School was always hard for me and my grades reflected it. My parents hounded and punished me for not trying hard enough. I did study and tried my best, but still I had trouble with school. Teachers told my parents I had the ability to get higher grades. No one gave it a thought that there might be a correlation between my poor eyesight and learning ability.

The summer after Pat graduated from high school, we moved to the newly built base housing in Sergeant Bluff. Mr. Lambert was my teacher in eighth grade and his family attended the same church we attended in Lawton. He knew our family for years. He took the initiative to investigate. He concluded my reading was behind my grade level due to my vision handicap.

When Mr. Lambert discussed it with my mother, I watched her reaction. She pursed her lips, crossed her arms across her chest, and said, "I don't believe it. We have his eyes tested every year and they tell us he can see just fine using one eye. If he would pay attention and quit playing around, he would do better in school." Mr. Lambert continued his appeal until Mother consented. Through his efforts, my reading and comprehension improved. In addition, by sitting up front in the classroom, it also helped my grades improve.

* * *

During those school years, the one thing I did enjoy was my music. It seemed learning and playing came natural. I was always one of the more proficient music students and practiced hard at home.

Morningside College in Sioux City offered a summer camp for exceptional music students. When I finished eighth grade, my music teacher arranged an invitation to the summer camp. My music teacher called my parents to get their permission. Mother thought it was nonsense, yet Dad consented. He delayed taking me to Uncle Hank's until after the camp.

The School of Music at the college and several members of the Sioux City Symphony conducted the camp. They gave small group and individual lessons. The college was seven miles from our house and every morning I got up early and rode my bike to attend the camp. Even when it rained, my parents never volunteered to drive me. I would throw on a military poncho my dad had given me and I would pedal like mad to arrive on time.

The three weeks ended with a combined concert with the students and the Sioux City Symphony. The concert was on the lawn of the college campus on Sunday afternoon. I was one of the few trumpet players who had a solo piece. Pat and her boyfriend attended, but neither of my parents did.

On the following Monday, Dad took me to Uncle Hank's for the rest of the summer. Each summer I brought my trumpet so I could continue to practice. One cousin played the clarinet, and another played the piano. When we could squeeze in the time, we would practice together.

As with the previous summer, Uncle Hank loved to tease. The practice of pranks and challenges continued. When my cousins and I did a job well, we received his praises. If we made a mistake, he was firm in correcting us, but never demeaning.

We worked hard sunrise to sunset. If we had a rainy period and got behind, we worked evenings using tractor lights. Although it was hard work, Uncle Hank and my cousins made it fun. We never worked on Sundays; we attended the small community church where Uncle Hank was an elder.

I don't remember exactly why; it could have been a rainy day. After we completed our chores, Uncle Hank went to the house and left us four boys to play in the barn. The barn was large enough to house all the dairy cows and other farm animals in the winter. The second floor was all hayloft and at the time was half full of newly baled hay. There was a bull being housed in a pen within the barn. The bull was mean and Uncle Hank warned me to never go into his pen. The hayloft had openings throughout the barn. They used them to drop hay down to feed the livestock during the winter.

My cousins and I were playing King of the Mountain and having a great time. We had been roughhousing, pushing and shoving each other off the stacked hay bales. My oldest cousin picked up a bale and tossed it at me. As I went to jump out of the way, I fell through one of the openings. I fell twenty feet from the loft landing into the bull's pen.

The fall knocked the wind out of me and I lay in the mud and manure attempting to catch my breath. "Oh – my – God" I said to no one. Desperately trying to breathe, I turned towards the bull. His eyes were fixated on me, and I thought, *He's going to kill me.* The spattering of manure was on my face, hair, hands, and clothes. The smell was – what can I say – it was bull manure. I remember my cousins hanging over the loft opening and hysterically laughing. I watched the bull move towards me, knowing if I didn't move quickly, I would be dead. Yet, I could not move.

When the bull was within arm's length, I reached out and started petting his head. He stopped, eyed me, and allowed me to continue petting him. Once able to breathe, I got up and crawled out of the pen. My cousins had came down from the loft and I joined them, laughing at the incident. Although, covered from head to toe in bull manure, somehow I was unhurt from the fall.

Aunt Ruth did not find humor in the incident, yet Uncle Hank could not stop laughing. Aunt Ruth scolded us for our horseplay. Before returning to the house for lunch, I had to hose off in the barn while my cousin brought me clean clothes. The rest of the summer they teased me about my encounter with the bull.

When it came time to return home, those old fantasies returned. *Oh, if Aunt Ruth and Uncle Hank knew what was going on, they would take me. I just know it.* The reality was if I asked them, they would want to know why. If I told them, then Dad would find out. I would be better off if I kept my mouth shut. I returned home depressed and worried about what awaited me this time.

Chapter 3 – The Conflict

"There was no one to tell
and nowhere to hide.
I kept the pain to myself
while part of me died."
- dotcomwomen

In the fall of 1961, I started my first year of high school in Sergeant Bluff. The school year began with a catastrophe. It was the first day and Freshman Orientation; I got sick. I spent hours in the bathroom and barely made it through the day. The next morning Mother took me to the doctor and they diagnosed me with mononucleosis. This is every teenager's nightmare, to have the "kissing disease." I ran high fevers, had delusions and nightmares. I missed the first two weeks of school before I was no longer contagious.

In November, they notified Dad the bomber wing was moving to Fairchild AFB, Spokane, Washington. I found out many of my base classmates from Sergeant Bluff would also make the move. Now the move and the changed school didn't seem as dreadful. Even though we had been at Sioux City AFB for six years, this upset Mother. Pat attended Morningside College and was living at home. Pat was engaged to her high school sweetheart and the move forced Mother and Pat's separation.

At Fairchild AFB, although old, there was enough base housing. We moved in as soon as our furniture arrived. Within weeks, my friends and I were comfortable with the change. I got involved in the band at the high school. Before the school year ended, I had challenged my way up to first chair of the trumpet section.

Because of our separate activities, I didn't feel the same tension at home. I was busy with school, my music, and after school activities. They gave Dad a change in duties, which required him extended hours at the office. Mother returned to her nursing and worked at the base hospital. Mother complained I was never at home. Dad told her to leave me alone as long as I wasn't getting into trouble. At the time, I never gave it much thought; I enjoyed my freedom.

The following summer it was too far for me to go to Uncle Hank's farm in Minnesota. I worked at the base commissary and bagged customers' groceries for tips. I had a good summer and I made good money. I spent several weeks with a school friend while my parents returned to Sioux City. They went to help Pat arrange and attend her wedding to Irwin. It upset Pat when I did not attend, but Dad told her it was more important for me to stay in Spokane and work. At the time, it did not matter to me. Being unrestrained, I was having too much fun.

A year later, Dad's bomber wing was now moving to Glasgow AFB, Glasgow, Montana. As you would expect, Mother was livid, "Bill, I'm not moving every year. If you don't do something, I swear I'll leave you and go back to Texas."

Many of the same group of friends who went to Spokane now moved to Glasgow. It helped to know I did not have to enter a new school alone.

Glasgow AFB had plenty of modern housing on base. The base was large; all the housing and facilities were new. The disadvantage — the base was over twenty miles away from the town of Glasgow. There was nothing between the base and town other than the rolling hills and a scattering of farms and ranches. The town of Glasgow was small and it had few amenities.

The base and its population were three times the size of the town. The base had an elementary school, but no high school. Every morning, I was up early to catch the school bus into town.

When I entered Glasgow High School, I faced something I had never encountered. I learned the townspeople resented the base's kids who dominated all the extra-curricular activities. If you wanted to play sports, band, etc. you had to excel to participate. For example, there were two bands in the high school. Anyone could be a member of the junior band. To be a member of the senior, or Scotty Band, you had to challenge your way in. The same was with sports. Base kids sat on the bench and watched lesser-qualified town kids play.

I joined the junior band and they placed me at third trumpet, last chair. I immediately started to challenge and within six weeks, I was first trumpet, first chair. The band director told me there was an opening in the trumpet section of the Scotty Band. He suggested I challenge for the position. He told me I had the talent and aptitude to make the band.

After Christmas break, I auditioned for the Scotty Band. I had practiced hard and I was confident. The committee consisted of three music teachers and four Scotty Band members. All had equal votes to determine the entry to the vacant positions. Sam held trumpet first chair in the Scotty Band. He told me he had listened to me play and he was anxious for me to join the trumpet section.

The day came and I was nervous. My weakness was site reading; however, I got a lucky break. The piece they handed me I had played in a regional competition two years before. I played it well. The next day when they posted the list of new band members, to my astonishment, my name was not on it. The selected trumpet player was a local kid I had challenged in the junior band and won his chair. Sam was on the committee and he swore the vote had been in my favor. I came home devastated. When I told Mother, she said, "I don't know where you thought you were so good they would give you a position in their band. It's your own fault. If you had practiced harder, you would have got in."

I was so upset over the rejection; I put my trumpet in the closet and did not play it for months. My parents never said a word. I was sure Dad wouldn't care; he was never a supporter of my music. Mother was the one who had to listen to me practice. In retrospect, she would have been happy for the silence.

After several months, at Sam's request, I joined his dance band. One of the guys taught me to play several chords on a bass guitar. Depending on the music, I would play trumpet, trombone, or the bass guitar. We played for teen dances on base and at the high school. We even played once at the officer's club on base. I am not sure how good we were, but we had a lot of fun and the dance floor was usually full.

My parents never inquired of my music again. Other issues took precedence. That year at Glasgow was the last time I practiced and played my trumpet. I have kept it all these years, and on an odd occasion, I would pull it out and try to play. I look back and wish I had not been so stubborn and selfishly proud. I loved my music and regret I gave it up.

* * *

In the spring of 1963, while we were still at Glasgow AFB, Granddad had a massive heart attack and died. I was devastated. I had loved him from the time I was a little boy; now he was gone. We drove out of our way to pick up Pat and her husband Irwin in Sioux City and continued non-stop to Mesquite for the funeral.

Dad's perception of grief was common among men. He said, "If men cry, they don't let others see it." Then he warned, "I do not want you acting like a crybaby. Besides, I need you to help me with your mother."

This was difficult for me and I would often have to go hide. As I stood at Granddad's casket, I refused to believe it was him. I asked, how could this happen? Of all the people in my life, Granddad was the only one who I understood loved me. Now what would happen?

The day of the funeral was a horrendous experience. When my mother, sister, and the rest of the family cried, I wouldn't allow myself. My dad was watching me and I was determined I wouldn't embarrass him or myself. When it came time to leave the cemetery, Dad had to pull me back to the car. I couldn't believe we had to put Granddad in the ground.

The family took Granddad's death quite hard. When it came time for us to return home, Mother announced to Dad and me, "I am not coming back with you. Grandma needs me now and I need to be with my family. I'm sure you two can survive on your own for a few weeks." Dad was unhappy, yet he didn't challenge her.

* * *

When we returned to Glasgow, the hostility at home returned. Dad was angry Mother wasn't there to prepare meals and maintain the house. It frustrated him due to his inability to do anything about it. He began to lash out and our confrontations ignited. I was also angered at Mother when I inherited many of the things she did on top of my normal chores. Evenings, Dad watched TV while I cooked, washed dishes, etc. When was I supposed to do my homework?

It was the end of my sophomore year and I had plans for the summer. I intended to return to work on Uncle Hank's farm. No way did I want to spend the summer alone with Dad. To my disenchantment, Dad said, "Get it out of your head, I'm not driving you over to Minnesota. You can find a job around here."

Dad did not cook because in his world it was "woman's work." Mother had taught me a few things and I would cook simple meals. Many evenings, we went to the Non-commissioned Officers (NCO) Club for dinner.

Dad's patience with me was short. One evening, I was cooking our dinner. He came into the kitchen. "What's taking so long? I expect my dinner to be on the table when I come home."

I lashed back, "I'm not Mother. I'm doing my—" Before I could finish my sentence, Dad hit me with his fist along the side of my face. I staggered back, and was about to say something when he slugged me again. This time I found myself on the floor.

As I began to sit up, he kicked me in the ribs. "I will not tolerate your smart mouth. Now get your ass up and fix my dinner."

I could taste blood in my mouth and my whole face throbbed. As he stood in the kitchen doorway, I finished preparing the meal. He sat at the kitchen table while I served him. He didn't say a word as I walked out to go to the bathroom.

When I looked in the mirror, my cheek had begun to swell. I also had a split lip and dried blood on my chin. I took a washcloth and cleaned the dried blood. I sat on the side of the tub trying to figure out what had happened. *Why did he use his fist? Why did he kick me? What did I do to deserve this? He's never done this before. Why now? All I was doing was cooking his dinner.*

I'm not sure how long I sat in the bathroom. Suddenly, the door flew open. "If you're not going to eat your dinner, then get in there and clean up the kitchen. I'm going out."

I was still in a state of confusion when he left and slammed the front door. I tried to eat, but my mouth was too sore. I put some ice on my face to stop the swelling. When I finished cleaning the kitchen, I went to my room. I was still in shock and couldn't believe this had happened. I closed my bedroom door, and turned off the lights as I went to bed.

It was sometime after ten o'clock when Dad came home. I lay in bed in fear he would come into my room. However, he went directly to his bedroom. I fell asleep but had a fitful night.

Over the next few weeks, we continued to have confrontations. He would slap or hit me with his fist, and if I went down, he kicked me. I would go to school with a bruised face and body. If asked, I would lie and say I had been in a fight with another boy. Dad's uncontrolled anger and the physical abuse were more than anytime in the past. I was taller and most likely as strong as Dad. I thought about fighting back. Yet, I was plain scared of him. I had been afraid from the time I was a little boy.

* * *

By the time school was out, I was desperate to find a way to leave home for the summer. I found out the farmers and ranchers in the area always hired high school boys for the summer. Even before school was out, I began my search. Even though we had an old Buick as a second car, I was only allowed to drive it on base. I found a local rancher who wanted summer help. I rode my bicycle twelve miles to interview for the job. I impressed the rancher, Charles McVee, when I rode my bike that far. To my elation, he hired me and I could start the next day. As I departed, he said, "Come on, put your bike in the back of the pickup. I will drive you back to the base." He instructed me to return with enough work clothes to last the week. "My wife insists when you come into the house for dinner, you have showered and changed clothes. You've got to have a pair of work boots; you can't wear those sneakers to work here."

Dad appeared pleased I had taken the initiative to go on my own and get the job. He helped me put together some work clothes and gave me a pair of his military boots. Dad drove me out to the ranch after dinner. On the drive, he said, "Make sure you show Mr. McVee you are a man and not a sissy boy. I'll be back Saturday night to bring you home for the weekend."

Even when I had obtained this job on my own, I thought he would show some pride in me. Instead, he still called me a sissy. What did I have to do to please him?

* * *

When Charles McVee, an only child, was in his twenties, he inherited the ranch when his dad died. That summer, Charles and his wife, Marlene, were both in their early thirties. They had a two-year-old boy and they were expecting their second child. Charles, with his heavy beard, always reminded me of the rough looking movie cowboys. He could do anything from repairing farm equipment to taking care of the ranch animals. Marlene was blond with fair skin, and taller and larger than her husband. She was not fat, just a big woman who, if necessary, could get out in the fields and work alongside the men. She was a very soft-spoken, loving wife and mother, and she was a great cook.

Their ranch was an average size for the area, but to me it was huge. They raised cattle, and each year, they would take the calves born in the spring and sell them in the fall to large feedlot companies. Charles told me the ranch was pie-shaped. It measured one-half mile at the south end, three miles at the north, and ten miles in length. The house, barn, corral, etc. along with the grain and hay fields were in the southern end. The southern end was in a valley with large creeks on either side. The north was on a plateau and used for the summer pastures.

Charles and Marlene, even when they had a prosperous ranching business, lived modestly. Their home was a small three bedroom, one bath, with a large kitchen. It was Charles' childhood home and his mother vacated it when he married. She had a mobile home located a few yards from the main house.

Even when I was just another high school boy, Charles and Marlene made me feel as if I was a member of the family. Charles was patient with me even when I made dumb mistakes. He loved to share stories of when he was a boy. He said he was often lonely being an only child. The closest playmate was over a mile away. As the summer progressed, I shared more with Charles and he became protective.

The only time I came into the house was for meals. Mornings, I was up before sunrise to milk the cows and do other chores. I would bring the milk to the house and wash up in a basin outside the kitchen door. I then joined Charles and Marlene for a huge breakfast. Marlene would bring lunch out to where ever we worked in the fields. There was no bunkhouse, so I slept on a rollaway bed on the screened in porch. They had a bathroom in the house, but I used the outhouse. Charles made a small outdoor shower next to the barn. After we milked the cows, completed the chores, and I had showered, we had dinner. After dinner, I retreated to the back porch where I read for a few minutes. But, often I was so tired, I was in bed and asleep by nine.

I worked harder that summer mowing and baling hay than any summer at my Uncle Hanks. Yet, I found it as memorable because of the escape from the stress at home. Charles told me once, "You remind me of myself when I was your age. I always wanted to do things the right way for my dad. If I messed up, he would walk away until he calmed down. Then he would explain what I had done wrong and how to do it right." Charles did the same with me; he never yelled or belittled me.

I had ridden horses before, but never one trained to work cattle. At least once a week, we rode to the north pasture to check on the cattle. I always enjoyed the distraction and the break from haying. One rainy day when we could not work, Charles took me into town. I purchased a pair of cowboy boots, which made it easier to ride. He also lent me a pair of spurs.

* * *

Saturdays were normally a shorter workday. Dad would drive out to get me and we would have dinner at the NCO club. Later in the summer, Dad started to let me drive the old 1953 Buick out to the ranch when he did not want to make the trip.

On Sundays, with Mother in Mesquite, Dad would mow the grass while I did his and my laundry. We would then clean the house. Dad was insistent that when Mother returned she wouldn't find the house in disarray.

It was during those Sundays at home, the arguments between Dad and me got even worse. I will admit there were times when I should have kept my mouth shut. As before, his anger was out of control, and he would hit me with his fist.

It was sometime in July, we had another confrontation and I ended up with a split lip, black eye, and very sore ribs. Afterwards, while I sat in my room, I made the decision I would not take his abuse anymore. I wrote a note, which stated he would never hit me again. I was leaving home and not coming back. Along with my work clothes, I packed some extra clothing and a few personal items. He was involved with something on TV; therefore, I went out my bedroom window.

I didn't have any plans of what to do or where to go. At that moment, I wanted to be anywhere but back home. When I couldn't decide where to go, I walked the twelve miles to the ranch.

As I walked to the ranch, I came up with a plan. I would tell Charles Dad went to Mesquite to get Mother. I was convinced he would let me stay there on weekends. With this lie, I could buy some time and avoid telling Charles the truth. With the money I earned through the summer plus my savings, I would have enough to be on my own. I would quit school and take off to anywhere my parents wouldn't find me.

It was after midnight when I got to the ranch. I went to the back porch to get some sleep. When the screen door accidently slammed, it woke Charles and he came out to check on me. He couldn't help but notice my split lip, swollen face, and black eye.

His face turned red, "What the hell happened to you?"

"It's okay. I don't want to talk about it."

"Did you get in a fight—or—did your dad do this?" He had seen the evidence before. Charles was insistent and I finally told him what had happened. "We will talk about it tomorrow." Yet, while we worked the next day, he said nothing. I was glad we didn't discuss it. I worried Charles might make me go home. What would I do then?

After dinner, Charles came to me, "I called your dad a few minutes ago. I told him I knew what he did. He denied it, but I told him I would call the sheriff if he ever hit you again. I also told him you could stay the rest of the summer at the ranch."

Charles surprised me; no one had ever interceded on my behalf before. I asked, "What did he say?"

Charles hesitated, "He said—uh—he didn't give a damn if you ever came back."

Even though my intentions were to run away from home, it upset me. I told myself, this proves what I always thought: he doesn't give a shit about me. He doesn't love me.

The more I thought about it, the more it angered me, and the more determined I was to not return home. From then on, Charles and Marlene rarely discussed my family. I spent the rest of the summer on the ranch. However, I had to plan something or I would have to go home.

During the day while I worked, my mind would drift. I kept reliving the past few months of the escalated abuse. I would attempt to determine what I had done wrong. I would ask myself, *Why didn't you fight back? It couldn't have been any worse if you had. Perhaps, he would have left you alone. It doesn't matter now; I'm not going back.*

Other than milking the cows, we did not work on Sundays. Marlene and Charles would go to church in Glasgow and then spend time with Marlene's family. They invited me, but I enjoyed the solitude and relaxation.

With permission, I would often saddle a horse and take a ride to explore areas of the ranch. Most of the watering holes in the north pasture were clear and spring fed. If the day was warm, I would go skinny dipping to cool off. I would milk the cows by myself, so Charles and Marlene didn't have to worry about what time they returned.

I started to fantasize what it might be like to stay with the McVee family. I also began to make my plans. Plan 'A' was to finish high school and work for Charles for my room and board. Plan 'B' was to run off to parts unknown. Neither plan was well thought out. With Plan A, I assumed Charles and Marlene would accept me living with them. What if they didn't? Plan B assumed I could survive on my own. I had no idea where I would go. Nevertheless, what was not in the plans was to return home.

Why should I go home? Dad doesn't care if I'm there or not. If I do go home, he will beat the shit out of me. I determined he would never do that again.

* * *

For the rest of the summer, I had no communication with Dad. The last week before school started, I got the nerve to ask Charles if I could stay with them and finish high school. He explained, "If we did, the law requires your parents' consent. You know as well as I do, that won't happen. Besides, with the new baby coming, I don't have room for you in the house." This disheartened me, yet Charles never said when I had to leave. Consequently, I started to think about Plan B.

Late afternoon of the same week, I spotted my parents' car pulling up to the house. I watched from afar as Dad and Mother talked to Marlene. Soon Charles joined the conversation. After a while, Charles came for me. "I know you saw your parents drive in. They want to talk to you."

"Tell them to go back home. I don't want to talk to them. I don't want anything to do with them."

I turned my back and started to walk away. Charles grabbed my shoulders, turned me around. "You've got to talk to them. You can't avoid this problem any longer. Look, nothing will happen. I promise you, no matter what happens, I won't let him hurt you."

I could feel my muscles tighten and I began to sweat. I wanted to argue, yet, I didn't know what to say. This wasn't what I had planned. At that moment, I wanted to run in the opposite direction. I had no alternatives, so I had to consent. We walked over to my parents; Marlene left and went into the house. However, Charles stood beside me.

Mother said, "Son, I am so sorry all this happened. Your dad regrets he lost his temper." Dad nodded his head but said nothing. "If I had been home, it would have not gotten out of control."

As she continued to make excuses for Dad and herself, I didn't pay attention. She was making the same excuses as before. She started her normal routine. Her lower lip started to quiver and then the crocodile tears started. "You know we love you and we only want the best for you. Blah—blah—blah."

She promised the fights would end. When Dad finally spoke, he did not sound apologetic. "I should not have taken my anger out on you. Things were tough for us all. Besides, you can't stay here; you need to go back to school."

All this time Charles had stood silently. He interjected, "Kenny, your parents are right, it is very important that you finish school. They have assured me you will be safe at home."

I didn't say anything. My mind went blank while I listened to each of their appeals. I was aware of the voices, yet I did not comprehend what was being said. I felt defeated.

After further promises and apologies from Mother, I consented to return home. With Charles at my side, I told Dad, "If you ever hit me again I will turn you in to the APs (Air Police)." Dad gave me a hard look, but said nothing.

After they left, I was so despondent, anytime Charles tried to talk to me I would say, "Please, please leave me alone." Nothing anyone could say would change things. I was convinced I was going back to the same hell.

Dad returned Saturday and I went home. Even when they promised, I was convinced the tension would start again. *Plan A and B have failed; I have no Plan C. What now?*

Mother went overboard to compensate for what had happened. She cooked some of my favorite foods. She promised me we would go shopping for new school clothes the next weekend. Dad said little and I avoided any lengthy discussions with them both. Then Monday, I started school.

* * *

I started my junior year of high school. Within a couple weeks, I began to enjoy the activities and friendships. I didn't focus on the turmoil from the previous summer. To compensate for what had happened, my parents allowed me more freedom to come and go as I pleased. When he was not using the old Buick, Dad allowed me to use it, even to drive into Glasgow for school functions. At first, there was this façade of happiness and interest in me. Within weeks, the old tension returned to the house. Mother and Dad argued daily and again I received the degrading comments. I avoided as much conversation or interaction with them as possible. I stayed away from the house or stayed in my room.

* * *

During my youth, periodically I would sleepwalk. My parents teased me when they recalled some of the weird things I did or places I would end up. One night, six weeks after school started, I had another episode. In my dream, I needed to find something in a cabinet. In reality, I was in my parents' bathroom and pulling things out of their medicine cabinet. I threw them on the floor, and broke some of the bottles.

I awoke on the floor of their bathroom with Dad standing over me. Before I could react, Dad grabbed me and began hitting me with his fist. "YOU STUPID BASTARD," he yelled as he continued to hit me. "WHAT THE HELL ARE YOU DOING?"

Mother was behind him and attempting to pull him off. She screamed, "BILL—STOP IT—STOP IT. YOU'RE HURTING HIM."

Although it was over quickly, I had a bruised face and a deep cut over my left eye.

Dad still stood over me while Mother tried to pull him out of the bathroom. She shouted, "BILL—WHAT IS THE MATTER WITH YOU? THERE WAS NO REASON TO HIT HIM. LEAVE HIM ALONE. DON'T MAKE ME CALL THE POLICE."

Dad turned toward her and it appeared he wanted to hit her. I jumped up and pushed him away. "Don't you dare touch her." He swung at me, but missed. Between the three of us, the threats and yelling continued until Dad dressed and left the house.

When he left, Mother took me into the bathroom to clean and look at the cut above my eye. She was able to get the bleeding to stop, but insisted I needed to go to the base hospital for stitches. Dad had taken one car and we could not find the keys to the other. She bandaged it and said we would go as soon as Dad returned or she could find the keys.

She started to apologize, but I interrupted. "I don't want to talk about it—please—just leave me alone—he promised he wouldn't hit me again. I haven't even been home two months—he did it again. Please—leave—me—alone!"

Mother continued to apologize and I didn't want to listen. I ran into my bedroom, slammed and locked the door. I was angry, yet I was crying. *I should have known better than to trust him. He doesn't give a shit about me. I never should have come home. I can't take this anymore. I am leaving and never coming back. That son of a bitch will never hit me again.*

I immediately started to pack my duffel bag. When I finished, there was nothing but silence in the house. Dad was still gone and I didn't care what Mother was doing. Again, I went out through my bedroom window. This time I didn't leave a note.

Chapter 4 – On the Run

"There are wounds that never show on the body that are deeper

and more hurtful than anything that bleeds."

—Laurell K. Hamilton

After midnight, underage dependents were not allowed off base. Since it was, I had to sneak by the guardhouse at the base entrance. When the guard wasn't looking, I ran across the road and hid. I then started my twelve-mile walk to the McVee's ranch. I was confused and didn't know where else to go. I was convinced Charles would take me in when he knew Dad had beaten me again. I would be safe there.

As I walked, each time car lights came in my direction, I would hide in the ditch or behind some bushes. My cut started bleeding and was running down my face. I used my handkerchief to wipe my face and get the bleeding to stop.

Why did Dad beat me this time – for sleepwalking? This can't be right. I don't remember saying anything to him. All I remember – when I woke up he was on top of me. There is no way I'm going back home. I know Charles won't make me go home.

It was early morning when I arrived and the sun was rising. I knocked on their kitchen door, Charles answered. Seeing my condition, he pulled me into the house. Before he could say anything, I was in tears and between sobs, I told him, "He did it again—he promised—I didn't fight with him—I was sleepwalking—Honest—"

Charles's face was red. "That—son—of—a—bitch! He said he wouldn't hit you again. I'm calling the Sheriff."

The cut above my eye started bleeding again. When Marlene looked at it, she insisted Charles take me to the hospital in Glasgow.

At the hospital, the doctor gave me several stitches and bandaged the area. While he worked on me, he was questioning how I acquired the injuries. I didn't want him calling my parents, so I didn't say anything. He kept repeating, "You need to tell me the truth. What happened?" I refused to tell him. After he finished, he went out to talk to Charles. I have always assumed Charles told the doctor how I had sustained the injuries.

We returned to the ranch and I fell asleep on the couch. It was afternoon when I awoke. Charles was out working somewhere on the ranch and Marlene was busy in the kitchen. She made me something to eat. As I ate, she inquired when the abuse started and what, if anything, did my mother do to protect me. If I told her the truth, there would be more trouble. I kept silent. Finally, she gave up. "Okay – we don't have to talk about it now. Charles is out on the south pasture mending fences, I'm sure he could use your help." She turned her back and returned to her work.

I drove one of the tractors out and found Charles. As with Marlene, he wanted to talk about my Dad's physical abuse. Rather than tell him the whole truth, I made excuses for Dad, still feeling scared what he might do.

Charles was insistent, "Your Dad can't be allowed to continue beating his family. The base authorities need to know what is going on. Do you realize he could have seriously hurt you or your mother?"

I interrupted, "Charles, you don't know him. He might not do anything now, but he will – "

"NO—I'm sorry—but no—something has to be done before he hurts anyone further."

I was shifting from foot to foot and I found it hard to look at Charles. *This isn't going away. No stalling or avoiding is going to make it better. What do I say to Marlene and Charles?*

We finished repairing the fence and did a few other odd jobs to stay busy. We finished the day with milking the cows and cleaning the barn. Even with the temperature dropping, I cleaned up, using the shower in the barn, and then came in for a hearty dinner. If my parents called looking for me, Marlene or Charles did not say. I had a feeling of false security, yet I had no idea of what I was going to do next.

I was to sleep on the couch again because it was too cold to sleep out on the screen porch. As the house got quiet, I could hear Charles and Marlene talking. Charles was insistent that the authorities, either at the base or the sheriff, be notified. He also wanted me to stay with them until things could be settled.

Marlene agreed with Charles on contacting the authorities, but she thought they should avoid interfering between the authorities and my family by taking me in.

The same thoughts kept replaying in my head: *Dad could get into trouble at the base. What if they demote him or kick him out. After he beats the shit out of me, he will kick me out of the house. It would be better I run now than to chance going back home. Will he come after Charles?*

I lay in the dark feeling the anxiety. One scenario led to another while the paranoia became intolerable. What little security I had, it quickly evaporated. It was a mistake getting Charles and Marlene involved. The longer I lay looking at the ceiling, the more I was convinced it was no longer safe here.

When the house was quiet and I was sure Charles and Marlene were asleep, I got dressed and grabbed my duffel bag. I stopped in the kitchen looking for something to write on. I found some scrap paper and wrote a note. "Sorry I didn't wake you. Please don't call the Base; Dad will come looking for you. I don't want you getting hurt. Thank you for everything you did for me."

I walked the eight or ten miles it took to get to Highway 2 (the main east-west highway). I continued just west of Glasgow to a truck stop where I started asking truckers for a ride. One trucker agreed and within minutes, we were heading west.

While walking, I planned to go to Spokane. I thought Mike, the classmate I had stayed with when Pat got married, might take me in. If that didn't work, I would go to California. I had seen a TV program where runaway juveniles went to Los Angeles. A Catholic church took them in and gave them protection. I would do whatever it took to never go back home.

The truck driver was friendly, yet he continued to stare at my bandaged face. "You're kind of young to be out here hitchhiking. You want to tell me what's going on. What happened to your face?"

"My older brother and I got into a fight," I lied. "I'm going to Spokane to live with my grandparents."

He didn't ask again. Yet, he kept looking at me with one eyebrow raised and his lips pursed. It was obvious he wasn't buying my story. When I kept falling asleep, he suggested I crawl back into the sleeper cab. I did and was asleep in minutes.

When I woke, we had traveled east on Highway 2 and then we went south. We were north of Butte, Montana and stopping at a truck stop. As I crawled out of the sleeper, I insisted, "Let me buy you breakfast. You were nice enough to give me a ride; it's the least

I can do." I persisted my offer and he politely declined. He wouldn't even let me buy him some coffee.

While we ate at a truck stop, he told me he would be continuing south. If I still wanted to go to Spokane, I needed to find another ride. He didn't have to say anything more. I could tell he was anxious to be rid of me. I thanked him and he drove off.

I started asking other truckers for a ride. Several took one look at me and refused. I got the idea that if I could hide my bandage and make myself look older, I would have a better chance. I purchased a trucker's cap, pulled it down low on my face, changed from my high school varsity athletic jacket into a blue jean jacket and my cowboy boots. I assumed the change helped, because I located a trucker going to Seattle, willing to drop me off in Spokane.

Like the first trucker, he questioned me about my age and my injury. I gave him the same lie. He too didn't buy it. Unlike the first trucker, he wouldn't accept my story. "I know you're lying, so why don't you just tell me the truth." When I continued my lie, he asked, "Are you running away from home?"

My body tensed and my legs begin to shake. He said, "I thought so. It can't be that bad at home." When I didn't answer he continued, "Who hit you—your Dad?" I didn't answer and just looked away. "If he did, you should go to the police. They will help you."

I couldn't stop shaking. Some of the same paranoid thoughts rushed through my mind. *What if he kicks me out of the truck? We are miles from town. No one is going to pick me up along this road. Should I tell him the truth? What if he turns me into the police?*

His face softened. "Look, it's none of my business. If you don't want to, you don't have to tell me anything. You are just too young to be out on your own. You need to get some help." He finally let the subject drop.

We headed west on what is now Interstate 90, traveling through the Rocky Mountains of Western Montana and Eastern Idaho. The roads were steep and often our speed dropped to navigate the sharp turns and quick changes of grade. After we had the tough mountains behind us, he stopped at a truck stop for fuel and a meal. He allowed me to pay for his dinner, but in return, he bought me cigarettes as he purchased some for himself. He pulled the truck over to the back of the truck stop to take a nap. I had the choice to wait with him or find another ride. Since I had a confirmed ride to Spokane, I leaned back in the seat and joined him in a nap.

When he woke up, we had some coffee and then headed west again. We arrived in Spokane in the late afternoon. I had been on the road for 36 hours and I was feeling more self-confident with my decision to run away from home.

* * *

When we stopped along side the road in Spokane, he again suggested I get some help. I thanked him for the ride, grabbed my duffle bag, and walked away. I began to worry he might call the police, so I wanted to disappear as quickly as I could.

I found a gas station about a mile down the road. I used the pay phone, found Mike's number, and called. When Mike answered, he thought I was calling from Glasgow.

I explained, "No, I'm in Spokane."

"What is going on? Did your Dad get reassigned back here?"

"Uh-uh. Mike, I ran away from home. I couldn't stand my dad beating the crap of me any longer, so I left."

"Where are you now?"

"I'm at a gas station on Highway 2. Not far from the base. Do you think I can stay a couple days with you?"

"Stay there and I'll come get you."

It was over a half-hour before he arrived. I sat out in the sun to keep warm and smoked. We sat in his Mother's car and I told him what Dad had done. He promised me he would ask his parents if I could stay with them. It didn't cross my mind they might call my parents. I had the false sense of security again.

I was welcomed at Mike's parents home and fed a great meal. After dinner, while I took a shower, Mike went to talk with his parents. When he returned, he told me he had just told them I was staying overnight. He promised he would talk with his mother tomorrow when his dad wasn't there.

The next morning I left with Mike. He went on to school and I started walking towards downtown. Mike told me to call him when he returned from school and he had an opportunity to talk to his mother. He kept reassuring me I would be able to stay with them.

I soon caught a ride and they dropped me off in the downtown area. As I explored, I found a Greyhound station. When I inquired about a ticket to California, the agent told me there was not an express bus until the next day. When he gave me the price, it was more than I had on me. If Mike's mother wouldn't take me in, then it meant I was back on the road hitchhiking.

I walked around and found a theater. I watched the movie twice, sleeping through most of it the second time. When it was five o'clock, I found a pay phone and called Mike. Mike quickly apologized but told me when his mother found out I had run from home, she refused to get involved. When I hung up with Mike, I was at a loss of what to do next.

I never gave it a thought, but the whole time I had been walking around the theater, I was carrying my duffle bag. I thought I would go back into the theater to think about what to do next. When I started in that direction, the manager stopped me. "I have been watching you. You have seen the movie at least twice. You can't be hanging out here. You are going to have to leave."

Walking out, the temperature had dropped and the downtown area shops were closing. I returned to the bus depot.

The depot had a small café; I sat down at the counter and ordered some coffee. There was a girl working about my age and she took my order. Between waiting on other customers, she began talking with me. I thought, as long as I am not forced to leave, I would stay. I wouldn't have to go out in the cold and later I could order some dinner. Beyond having dinner, I had no idea where I would go next. I speculated I could always catch a bus west to Seattle. I had enough money for a ticket there.

At ten o'clock, the café closed. I walked outside only to discover the temperature had dropped more. I walked back in and found a quiet area away from the ticket windows and the departure doors. Around midnight, I stretched out using my duffel bag as a pillow and fell asleep. I would wake up briefly from the noise of bus arrivals or departures. No one bothered me so I stayed on my bench the remainder of the night.

The next morning, when the cafe opened, I returned for a vigil of conversation and coffee. During the afternoon, I found a bank and after extensive haggling, the manager finally agreed to cash my check from the credit union at Glasgow Air Force Base. With the money I now had, I could purchase a ticket to Los Angeles. However, this would leave me nothing to live on.

It hit me when I left the bank. *You stupid jerk, by cashing the check, Mother and Dad are going to know you are in Spokane. Now what? It will only be a matter of time before the police find me. What I need is a job and somewhere to live where they can't find me. When I have more money, then I can go to California.*

Again, I wasn't clearly thinking. I never thought about getting a job without revealing my identity. Even if I got a job, who would let a seventeen-year-old boy rent an apartment or room. I looked more like fifteen than seventeen. Where was I going to hide where the police wouldn't find me? These and more were examples of immaturity.

In 1963, life for a teenage boy was different than today. Perhaps boys are more mature and aware of their world than I was at that age; nonetheless, seventeen-year-old boys should not be living on the street. To be caught and forced to return home was my biggest fear. I was still seeking the individual who would love me. I was living in fear and following some kind of instinct to survive.

* * *

After leaving the bank, I started walking aimlessly. When it began getting dark, I returned to the bus station. At the bus station, I rented a locker for my duffel bag. My immediate plans were to try to spend the night again at the bus station. I went directly into the café, where I noticed the teenage girl from the previous night was there.

As we did the night before, we sat talking between her waiting on customers. I introduced myself. "My name is Robert Sloan. But everyone calls me Bobby," I lied. She told me her name was Linda.

She kept my coffee cup filled and later in the evening she asked, "Are you hungry? Our cook will make you a plate from leftovers and it won't cost you anything".

I gave a dismissive snort. "I can pay for my meal."

She interrupted, "Look, it is none of my business, but you're not the first boy to hang out here when they didn't have any money or a place to go. Besides, Larry gives all of us leftovers. What isn't eaten, he has to throw it away."

Although I was embarrassed, I consented. After a few minutes, a tall thin black man came out of the kitchen with a plate. I thanked him and volunteered to help him clean up in the kitchen. He declined my offer, telling me he could get in trouble by allowing someone not employed into the kitchen. "Besides," he said, "I gots me a helper in the back who washes dishes and cleans."

Linda asked about my injuries. Since she was my age, I assumed I could trust her. I told her I had run away from home, but I didn't tell her how I was injured. I also told her of my plans to find a job and rent a room.

She said, "I know the manager of a Piggly Wiggly grocery store. He is a neighbor and I babysit for him. He is always hiring high school kids. If you want, I will call him tomorrow." I told her I had experience working at the commissary on base.

When the café closed and Linda left, I went over to my spot and spent the night on the bench. The prospect of getting a job raised my optimism, yet I had a restless night.

The next morning I cleaned up, using the sink in the men's room. Once the café opened, I went in and ordered coffee and something for breakfast. I found a newspaper and I started looking at the employment ads. Later in the morning, the counterwoman came over and asked, "Are you Bobby?"

"Yes ma'am."

"You have a phone call from Linda."

Linda told me she had talked to Mr. McKinley, the grocery store manager. If I could be at his store after one o'clock, he would talk with me. She gave me directions to the store and it was a several-mile walk. I went to my locker, grabbed my jacket, and started out.

When I found the store, I went in and located the office. I asked to speak to Mr. McKinley. He was paged and when he arrived, he said, "Hello. I'm John McKinley, are you Bobby?"

"Yes sir," I replied as I shook his hand.

I followed him to the back and he found a quiet area in the warehouse, where we sat on wooden crates. He first asked about my job experience. I told him about my commissary job and working on farms most summers. He explained the job duties, the pay of a $1.25 per hour and the hourly limitations for minors. He asked, "Do you go to school?"

"Not right now. But I want to go back and graduate." Not thinking I added, "When I get a job and a place to stay, I'll be able to go back to school."

"By the way, where are you sleeping at night?"

Linda had told him where I was staying. There was no reason to lie. "I've been sleeping at the bus station." I kept waiting for him to ask about my bandaged face, but he never did.

He guided me back upfront to the office to fill out a job application. On the walk upfront, my mind was racing, wondering what I would put on the application. *What if they check? I won't get the job when they find out that I lied.*

The form was simply asking for my basic information. I used the name Robert Sloan and our previous address and telephone number when we were living on Fairchild Air Force Base. When I handed in the form, Mr. McKinley told me to return tomorrow at five o'clock to begin working. I couldn't stop smiling while I repeatedly thanked him before I left.

I started walking to the bus station, telling myself if I got a job this easily, I should be able to find a room to rent too. I was convinced I was starting a new life and I would never have to go back home. As I walked, the fantasies went wild. In my fantasy, I had a great apartment, had enough money to buy a car, started dating Linda, and went back to school. Everything was perfect and no one was aware of my past. I returned to the bus depot optimistic my world was changing and I would be secure.

When Linda came into work, she was pleased I got a job, but expressed her concern for me sleeping at the bus station. Later the cook brought me a plate of food and he too expressed his concern for my safety. He suggested I go to the YMCA or the Salvation Army, since they provided temporary shelter.

That evening, I discovered a cot in the back of a storage room in the men's restroom. Instead of sleeping on the bench, I locked myself into the storage room and slept on the cot.

The following morning, after breakfast, I obtained directions and walked to the YMCA. There was an information desk and I inquired on room availability.

After giving me a visual assessment, he affirmed, "Yes, we have a dorm, but minors aren't allowed to stay there. You would have to stay in a private room. Call me after five o'clock and I will know if I have a vacancy. Oh, by the way our rates are one dollar per night or five dollars per week."

I gave him my name, wrote down their phone number. I was about to leave when he offered me the opportunity to use their facilities for a shower. I accepted his invitation and it was great having a hot shower and feeling clean. *I wished I had known and I would've brought clean clothes.*

It was early, the day was warmer, and I was feeling confident. I started my walk to my new job and stopped on my way for some lunch. I got impatient for five o'clock and walked into the store thirty minutes early. I found Mr. McKinley and he introduced me to Mrs. Carroll, the Assistant Manager. Mrs. Carroll was about thirty years old, very petite with blond hair and wearing a store jacket. As he introduced me, I noticed her beautiful green eyes.

She escorted me to the employees' lounge and locker rooms. I was issued a couple of store shirts and a locker. After changing into my store shirt, I returned up front to get my assignment. Mrs. Carroll introduced me to a couple of the cashiers and Tom, a boy my age. She told Tom to get me oriented and instructions on their way of bagging groceries. Turning to me, she said, "Your primary responsibility is to the cashiers and keeping up with them."

The store was not busy and I had no trouble catching on to their procedures. During my break, I called the YMCA. The attendant apologized; he had nothing, but advised me to check with them daily.

I hung up thinking I would have to spend another night at the bus station. I thought, *Sleeping in the janitor's closet was not bad. At least it was warm and more comfortable than sleeping on the benches.* I returned to the front and resumed bagging groceries and helping customers. I was surprised when they announced the store would be closing in five minutes. After closing, I helped sweep and mop the area around the checkout stations.

Mrs. Carroll came over to me and said, "Since this is your first day, it won't be necessary for you to stay and help stock shelves. Oh yes, Mr. McKinley is waiting for you in the employee lounge. You have a good night and I'll see you tomorrow afternoon."

I headed to the back to find Mr. McKinley. I couldn't help but worry he had discovered I lied on my application. I found him sitting at the table drinking a Coke. "Hi Mr. McKinley, you wanted to talk to me?"

"Yes, Bobby. Linda called me and said she was worried because you are sleeping at the bus station. Is this true?"

"Yes, but now, I have a job; I'm sure I can find something soon. I tried the YMCA, but they were full. I'll look again tomorrow."

He paused and replied, "Look, I talked with my wife and we would like you to stay at our house tonight."

Defensively I thought, *Why is he being nice to me? Is this a set up to call the police?* I didn't listen to my inner voice. My voice broke as I answered, "Thank you Mr. McKinley—I really do appreciate it."

He smiled and said, "Come on Bobby, let's get out of here. My wife, Marianne, was making us something to eat when I left the house. She is anxious to meet you."

I followed him out the back door and got into his car. His house was not more than a couple of miles from the store. As we pulled into the driveway, I was surprised at how small the house was, yet it looked warm and inviting. I followed him up the steps and into the house.

Marianne was waiting. She was petite with long brown hair and hazel eyes like mine. She was beautiful. She caught me staring at her. I quickly looked away, blushing and feeling embarrassed.

I followed John and Marianne to the kitchen. We sat at a small table in the corner where Marianne served us soup and sandwiches. When they did not ask any personal questions, I started relaxing. Marianne told me they had a little boy about three years old, John, Jr. She giggled, "He sometimes is an early riser and hopefully he won't wake you too early."

When we finished, John led me to the basement. There was a laundry area located adjacent to the stairs, and towards the front of the house was a small family room. There was a couch and a couple of matching chairs, lamps on tables, and a coffee table in the center. Off to one side was a small TV on a stand. John showed me a small bathroom with a shower over by the laundry area. Marianne had made up the couch with sheets, a pillow, and a blanket. With the furnace unit in the same room, it was cozy and warm.

Before leaving, John said, "Make yourself comfortable and if you need anything just let me know. Do you think you will be okay down here?"

"Thanks, Mr. McKinley — this is great."

John went up stairs and I sat down in the chair. There was evidence of John smoking in the house and there was an ashtray on the coffee table. I pulled my jacket off and got my cigarettes. I turned on the TV and Johnny Carson was on. After a few minutes, I began getting sleepy. I crawled into bed and woke the next morning hearing a little boy's voice upstairs.

In the bathroom, Marianne had left towels, soap, and shampoo. After a shower, I went upstairs to find Marianne and Junior in the kitchen. When John walked in, the three of us sat together with Junior having our breakfast. Although cautious, I had a feeling these people were genuine and compassionate. Although not as rugged as Charles McVee, John's temperament was very similar. Both were protective of their family, yet at the same time they were compassionate towards me.

After breakfast, John looked at me and said, "How about we go downstairs and have a talk."

We refilled our coffee cups and headed downstairs. He said, "Linda told me you have run away from home. She said you are scared the police will find you and you will have to return home. She did not say how you got injured, but we can talk about it another time."

I instantly tensed and my right leg began to shake. I told myself, *I shouldn't have stayed here last night. He is going to call the police.* I took a deep breath, "Mr. McKinley, I can explain—"

"Just a minute, Bobby," he insisted. "What I want to do is help you without getting my wife or myself in trouble. We are willing to give you a safe place to stay until we can get this sorted out. However, we cannot hide you if your parents come looking for you. Understand?"

"Yes sir." The sweat popped out on my forehead and now both legs were shaking. *What do I do now?*

He broke my thoughts: "We cannot help you if you lie to us.

With my head down to avoid eye contact, I told him my dad had always been abusive. But lately it got worse. "I couldn't stand it anymore, so I took off." After my shower the day before, I hadn't covered the cut above my eye. It was healing, yet the stiches were visible.

I could feel his eyes on me, "Is that how you got the cut above your eye? How long ago did this happen?"

I whispered, "About a week ago."

"Why did you come to Spokane? Do you have relatives here?"

"No sir, my dad is in the Air Force and we were stationed here about a year ago. I thought one of my high school friends might give me a place to stay."

The sweat was running down my back. I tried to slow down my breathing. *Oh shit, do I run again?*

Seeing my reaction, his voice softened. "Bobby, come on. I really want to help you. I want you to feel you can trust me."

When I looked up, he had a sympathetic look. "I think our pastor can give us advice on how to handle this and still protect you. I promise I won't give him your name. Do I have your permission?"

I was hearing his voice, but my whole body was shaking now. I said nothing. I just nodded my head yes.

"Linda told me you had a duffle bag with your stuff at the bus station. Let's go down there and get it."

When we finished, he went upstairs to talk with Marianne. As I sat there, I was still debating whether to stay or run. The body shakes ceased and my breathing returned to normal. I grabbed a cigarette and lit it.

In few minutes, he yelled down to me, "Okay Bobby, let's get going."

We headed downtown to the bus station and I retrieved my duffle bag. As I walked out of the bus station, I thought, *I hope I never see this place again.*

Chapter 5 – A Safe Place

"The Wounded Child has been trained to always be vigilant,
for there could be unexpected cruelty at any moment or any time.
Hyper-vigilance keeps us in a constant state of stress."

Posted by Woody Haiken
woundedchildsjourney.com

I had now been away from home almost a week. I went from virtually living on the street to having a safe haven. I went from limited funds to having a source of income. I had allowed John and Marianne McKinley to take me into their home. I was so desperate for someone to accept me; I disregarded my fear of the police catching me.

I ignored any consequences from allowing the McKinleys to take me in. I convinced myself these were good people and they wouldn't harm me. I believed I could evade my parents and the police. Everything was going to be okay. Yet, I had this pessimism I couldn't shake.

As promised, working at Piggly Wiggly had me in the warehouse, stocking shelves, or bagging groceries. I caught on quickly to the responsibilities of each area of the job and Mrs. Carroll in turn gave me praise. Each day, I lost myself in my work, and gave little thought to my past. At the end of the next week, Mrs. Carroll handed me my first paycheck.

The store cashed my paycheck and I immediately gave John a part to pay for my expenses in their home. During the week, I ran into Marianne more than I did John. His schedule was opposite mine. We would speak briefly at work as I began and he was leaving. Most evenings, he was upstairs when I would return from work. They trusted me enough to give me a key to the house, giving me freedom to come and go as I pleased. Every night when I returned from work, Marianne had leftovers or a sandwich left out for me. She washed my clothes and left them folded on the coffee table downstairs.

Any time I had a conversation with either John or Marianne, they were not questioning me about my past. I felt as if I belonged in their home. I wanted to please them and when it appeared I had, the black cloud disappeared to sunshine. I was feeling happiness again — something I hadn't felt in a long time.

The second Sunday I was there, John told me his mother was a nurse. He told her about my stitches and she suggested John bring me out to her house to remove them. He explained his parents owned a dairy farm a few miles from Spokane. I agreed and John and I left after they returned from church.

We drove south of Spokane to his parents' farm. The house reminded me of Aunt Ruth and Uncle Hank's house, a white three-story house with attic dormers. A red barn was set back to the left of the house with an attached large silo. There were several other small buildings housing the farm equipment. A pair of beautiful collie dogs greeted us barking and showing excitement. They recognized John's car.

As we pulled up, a short and stout woman came out of a side door and walked in our direction. She had beautiful white hair and a big smile on her face. "Hello John," she said. John went to greet his mother, giving her a hug and kiss. Watching from the car, I witnessed this expression of love between mother and son. I was envious of what I witnessed. John signaled me to join them.

After he introduced me to his Mother, she led me to the kitchen where she had set out medical instruments and supplies. After she looked at the area, she removed the stitches. She put some ointment on the area, and gave me the rest of the tube, instructing me to use it twice a day. I thanked her and left looking for John.

I found John and his father in a building next to the barn. John introduced me to his father. I said, "Glad to meet you Mr. McKinley. I really like your farm. It reminds me of my uncle's farm."

"Where's your uncles farm?" he asked

"His place is in Warren, Minnesota. It is in Northwest Minnesota near the Red River area. This was the first time I had mentioned any area of the country I had lived.

John was quick to notice. "Minnesota, is this where you were living when you left home?"

"No. I worked there several summers and always enjoyed my uncle's farm. He had dairy cattle too, but he was a big potato farmer. My dad came from around the Park Rapids area. Are you familiar with that area?" Neither man said they were familiar with Park Rapids.

To avoid answering more questions, I asked permission to look around the farm. With no objections, I left to explore the farm. For the next hour, I walked around looking in the barn and then proceeded out to the adjacent pasture and woods. I was on my way back when I recognized John calling me. I quickly returned toward the house.

He was waiting for me and announced, "Look, if we don't leave now, then Pop will want us to help with the milking. Then my mother will want us to stay for supper."

I said, "I'm enjoying being out here on the farm. It would be fun milking the cows."

"I wouldn't mind staying if Marianne and Junior were here too. But I want to go back home now."

We walked back to the house, said our goodbyes, and headed back towards town. Once in the car, John started with the questions. "You said your dad was from Minnesota. You have also told me he is in the military. Where is your dad stationed now?"

As before, when he started asking questions, my body tensed and my heart rate quickened. "I promised I wouldn't lie to you. It's—I'm scared—do we have to talk about my family?"

"I understand this scares you, but you are only seventeen. You should be back in school. If the police were aware it was dangerous for you to return home, they would place you somewhere safe."

The red flag of mistrust was flying again. I was silent for several minutes. "John, I know you want to help. But if the police get involved, how do I know they will believe me and not my parents?"

"Has anyone ever confronted your parents, especially about your dad's abuse?

"I don't think so." *Why is he asking those questions?* Then I remembered what Charles McVee had said. I continued, "The man I worked for over the summer witnessed the last two beatings. He told me he was going to report my dad. That is when I took off and ended up here in Spokane."

"That should tell you what your dad did was wrong. If your parents have reported you as a runaway, then the police will find you. If you will go to them first, then they will investigate the situation. If you are in danger, they won't force you to go home."

"Please—please!" My body began to shake inside and the sweat popped out on my forehead. "I don't know—you and Marianne have been so nice—"

John interrupted. "I wish there was something I could say to convince you to trust me."

I was trying to stop my body from shaking. When the tears escaped, I looked out the window to avoid looking at John. Neither of us spoke the remainder of our drive to John's house.

When we arrived at the house, I went straight downstairs. While I sat smoking, I thought, *If I go to the police, will Dad get in trouble? Will they kick him out of the Air Force? Will they put him in jail? I do not want that, but I don't want him hitting me either. Should I pack my stuff tonight and get out of town?*

John interrupted my thoughts, "Hey Bobby, supper is ready. Come on up"

I was not hungry but I replied, "Okay, I'll be right up."

We spent supper talking about my enjoyable afternoon visiting the farm. After supper, John and I cleaned up the kitchen while Marianne went upstairs to put Junior to bed. I spent the night tossing and turning with indecision. I kept going over John's suggestion of going to the police. I couldn't convince myself the police would believe me over my parents. *Mother will do her crying act and convince everyone I had run away without a reason. Dad will lie to protect himself with the Air Force. Yet, if I run, I will be on the streets again. I do have a warm and safe place here. Can I trust the McKinley's?*

I woke up the next morning just as confused.

The next week went by quickly with me volunteering to work late every night. I purposely avoided John and Marianne by not returning to the house until I thought they would be upstairs in bed. I slept in on Sunday morning. When I heard the family came home from church, I purposely avoided coming upstairs.

The door opened and John came down. "Bobby, I think it is important we talk again." He told me he had talked to his pastor and to both his and Marianne's parents. Everyone had agreed if I were in danger, the police would protect me. He paused and looked straight at me. "We can't help you further until you tell us everything. I hope you understand."

I wanted to trust John, but there was this little voice saying—NO. My confusion and indecision was as great as ever. Perhaps it was the look on John's face or the sincerity in his voice. After several minutes of listening to John's attempts to convince me, I made the decision to trust him. I took a deep breath, "Okay John, ask your questions."

He exhaled and his face relaxed. "I want you to know, no matter how this ends up, I won't let anybody put you in danger."

We both grabbed our cigarettes and lit them. He began, "Tell me where you were living before you came here?"

"We were at Glasgow Air Force Base. It is in Montana."

"I know what you put down on the application sheet at the store. But tell me how old you are and did you give the store your correct social security number?"

"That information is correct except for the address and phone number. I put down where we lived at Fairchild." I thought,

If he doesn't ask, I am not telling him my real name. If I have to run, he will still think I'm Bobby Sloan.

When he asked about the cut over my eye and the bruises, I told him about the sleepwalking incident and the other previous beatings. When he asked about my relationship with my mother, I told him she had made feeble attempts to protect me, but she really didn't care. I continued explaining they had adopted me, and I had never felt loved by my parents.

He asked, "Didn't you ever tell anyone what went on at home? How about your Aunts or Uncles? Did your grandparents know anything about it? Did you ever go to one of your teachers at school?"

"No, I would never tell anyone. Dad threatened me with more punishments if he found out I told anyone." I kept telling myself, *Only answer the questions he asks. Don't volunteer anything.* It confused me not knowing where this was going. I wasn't shaking, yet the sweat was pouring down my back and the side of my face. I grabbed my handkerchief and wiped the sweat from going into my eyes. My mind was racing and the internal argument to stay or to run was back.

When he finished his questions, he asked permission to talk again with his pastor and parents. I said, "Please try to understand; it's hard for me to trust anyone completely. If it wasn't for Marianne and you, I would still be on the streets."

After John went upstairs, I still had this feeling of distrust. That inner voice was saying, *Run while you have a chance. Pack your duffle bag and get the hell out of here.* Even when everything was indicating otherwise, I made the decision to stay. I stayed because I wanted to believe John would help and protect me.

* * *

It was the following Thursday evening; I was stocking shelves in the store. I was concentrating on getting the cans of vegetables placed on the shelves in perfect alignment. As I was kneeling on the floor and working on the bottom shelves, I heard a voice addressing me, "Hey Ken—hey Ken Johnson." I instinctively turned towards the voice where stood a man in a suit and tie. "Your name is Kenneth Johnson, isn't it?" I stayed kneeling on the floor. Instantly, my body went rigid. I did not say a word, but stared at him. "Would you mind standing up?"

I did as requested, still not saying a word. I could feel my heart banging and my body starting to shake uncontrollably. Every fear I had felt over the last few weeks came rushing back at me.

"My name is Detective Andersen and I'm with the Orchard County Sheriff's Department." He pulled a case from his inside coat pocket and displayed his badge. "Is your full name Kenneth Wayne Johnson?" I unconsciously started looking around to assess whether anyone was watching. "Son, you need to answer my questions. Do not make it tough on yourself. Once again, is your name Kenneth Wayne Johnson?"

My voice squeaked, "Yes Sir." The body shakes continued and my mind was racing. *What do I do – oh my God – what do I do?*

"Calm down. You are not in trouble. Is there somewhere privately we can go to talk?"

"Can—can I get Mr. McKinley to be with me?"

"Who is Mr. McKinley?"

"Mr. McKinley is the store manager." The detective gave me an affirmative nod.

The detective accompanied me toward the office and I found Mrs. Carroll. "Is — uh — is John — I mean — uh — Mr. McKinley still here?"

She said, "No, he went home over an hour ago." She looked at me and then at the detective. "Is there a problem, Bobby?"

I did not answer, "Can — can I use the phone? I need to talk to Mr. McKinley — now." I followed her to the office. When I tried to use the phone, I was shaking so much she had to dial it for me.

Marianne answered. "Marianne — is John — there? PLEASE — I got to talk to him."

She yelled for him and he was quickly on the phone. "Hello."

"John — I need your help! There's a policeman here — I'm scared; can you come here?"

"Of course, what's going on?"

Not wanting to explain, I handed the phone to the detective. Detective Andersen was talking, but my mind was racing and I didn't comprehend what was being said. I couldn't get my body to stop shaking. Mrs. Carroll was looking at me, but I avoided eye contact. My mind said — RUN, yet my feet wouldn't cooperate. I gave no explanation to Mrs. Carroll other than to tell her I had to leave with him. I didn't tell her who he was or where we were going.

John suggested, and the detective agreed, to come to the house. After changing out of my store shirt, we went out the back. When we got to the house, John was waiting outside. "Officer, would you mind telling me what this is about?"

"This young man is listed as a runaway juvenile. The report stated there was a chance he was in the area. We followed a couple of leads and found him working at the store where I am told you are the manager. I need to ask him a few questions. Ken asked if you would be present. Are you all right with that?"

John looked at me, "Your name is Ken? I had a hunch you—"

I interrupted, "I'm sorry, John. I never lied to you. You never asked me what my real name was, so I never told you."

The detective spoke up, "Are you all right being present when I talk with him. If not, I can take him downtown."

"No, it's not a problem. Let's go inside." John led us into the house and down the stairs to the basement. Detective Andersen started by asking me how long I had been here in Spokane and how I got here. When he asked about my living with the McKinley's, John spoke up, "I found him living at the bus station. I gave him a job and place to stay."

The detective returned his look to me. "Why did you run away from home?"

"Do I—uh—have to tell you?" My body was still shaking and I had soaked the back of my shirt with sweat.

John interrupted, "Yes you need to tell the officer why you're scared and why you left home."

I reached into my jacket pocket, grabbed and lit a cigarette. I offered one to John and he took it. "My dad was beating me. I couldn't take it any longer, so I left home."

John spoke up, "When I first met — Bobby — uh — Ken, he did have a large cut above his eye with stitches. His face was still bruised. His father scares him and he worries about the safety of his mother."

The detective continued, "What does your father do back in Montana?"

"He is a Master Sergeant in the Air Force and stationed at Glasgow Air Force Base."

"To your knowledge has he ever been in trouble for fighting or hitting your mother or you?"

"I don't think so." The room started to spin and then I was sliding off the couch. John grabbed me and helped me sit back on the couch. I was gasping for air and my heart was pounding. I unknowingly said out-loud, "Oh my God, Dad is going to kill me if he gets into trouble at the base."

The detective did not reply. He was intensively watching me. "I know you are scared, but you need to calm down. No one here is going to hurt you."

Both John and the detective instructed me to take deep breaths. As I did, I began to calm down, yet I was still shaking inside. When the detective observed my breathing returning to normal he continued, "I want you to go with me downtown to our offices. I need to make a few calls and confirm your story. If you are telling me the truth, then we will need to take whatever steps are necessary to protect you."

I leaned forward and my voice broke, "Please — please believe me. I'm telling the truth. Please believe me." As my mind raced, I looked at John and then at the detective. "Can John come with me?"

The detective paused, drew a deep breath, and said, "If you are in danger, then it is my job to protect you. No, I do not think we need to involve Mr. McKinley further. He verified your story."

The detective came over and took hold of my arm with authority. He forced me to stand, led me out of the house, and placed me in the back seat of the car. He didn't even give me the opportunity to say anything to John or Marianne. We proceeded to drive down town to the courthouse and the sheriff's office. On the drive, I gave him Charles McVee's name. I told him I had worked for him all summer and he would verify my dad had beaten me.

Sitting in the back seat, everything I had feared was coming true. For the last hour, my anxiety was out of control. Now my fear was turning to anger. *When John started asking questions, I should have run. How stupid can I be for trusting anyone? Now, I'm going to have to go back home.*

The detective put me in a room and locked the door as he walked out. I thought, *If Detective Andersen calls Charles, he will tell him the truth.* The fantasies began. *Maybe I won't have to go back. I'll bet they will let me stay with John and Marianne. I can go back to school. John and Marianne will love me, I just know it, and all my dreams will come true.*

I waited for the longest time, what felt like hours. The longer I waited the more pessimistic I became. What kept repeating in my mind was I would be going home only for Dad to beat me again. *If they do, I am going to run. This time I will be more careful.* A uniformed officer checked in on me and escorted me so I could use the restroom.

Finally, Detective Andersen came into the room and sat down. "I have talked with the Sheriff's office in Glasgow and they told me Mr. McVee filed a report with them. I called Mr. McVee and he verified your side of the story. I called Glasgow Air Force

Base and talked with a Colonel Sullivan. He is aware of your family problems. He told me your dad received counseling and he knows this can not happen again."

I could tell from his voice he wasn't going to give me good news. He continued, but my heart sank. "When you go back, the Air Force people will be monitoring things. You don't have to be scared."

As he said, "When you go back," any hope I had previously was now gone.

I will have to start all over again. This time I will plan it better. I will make sure I have plenty of money before I leave. I will go somewhere different, somewhere they won't think about finding me.

Then he said, "I also called and talked with your Mother. She was very happy we found you and you are safe. In fact, she was crying…"

I interrupted, raising my voice, "She always cries. She thinks if she cries, we will forgive her." Raising my voice further, I fumed, "Shit — nothing is going to change. You are going to make me go home only for Dad to beat the crap out of me again." I stood up and pointed my finger at him. "If you make me go home, I'll only run again!"

He stood, took my shoulders, and forced me to sit. "Settle down, that's not going to help." He paused. "The authorities at the base and the Sheriff's office will get my report. I told your mother the base authorities would be monitoring the situation in your home. I told her the conditions of your return meant the physical abuse could never happen again. She promised me you would be safe. Under these circumstances, I'm required to return you to your parents."

My anger quickly changed to defeat. There was no way I believed him. There had been so many years of fear and abuse. There was no way Dad would change. My body started to shake again. "So, what happens next?"

"I need to make arrangements to have you sent back to your parents." He paused. "Since it's obvious we can't trust you, I will assign an officer to go with you. He will ensure your safe return to Glasgow."

"It's obvious you don't give a shit—"

"Ken—you aren't the first boy I have helped. Maybe I am not making myself clear. The authorities on the base will be watching to make sure you are safe. I'm telling you, it is in your best interest to go home, return to school and graduate from high school. If your dad even makes a threat towards you or your mother, call the police. Understand? Now, will you act like a gentleman and go back peacefully?"

I thought, *He is full of crap. Dad is not going to change. Mother and Dad will make sure everyone thinks everything is okay. But it won't be. It will be the same old shit. The detective can send me back, but that doesn't mean I will stay.*

I agreed to go home without fighting; although, I was not convinced I would be safe. He suggested we go back to the McKinley's house and get my things. "This will give you an opportunity to thank them. I think they are special people. Not everyone would take a seventeen-year-old runaway into their home." On the drive, he explained I would return by train.

When we arrived, John and Marianne met us at the door. The detective stood by the basement door talking with John and Marianne. I took a quick shower and packed my things into my duffel bag.

When I returned upstairs, Marianne took both my hands in hers. She said, "You might not understand now, but this is the best thing for you. You need to go home and finish high school." John shook his head in agreement. Marianne's eyes filled with tears and John was avoiding eye contact. While trying to hold back the tears, I made a feeble attempt to thank them for everything they had done. Finally, I couldn't look at their sad faces any longer. The damn broke, my tears began and I choked back a sob. I grabbed my bag and ran out the door.

John and Marianne encouraged me to call them if I needed to talk to someone. It was something I never did. The first year I wrote them several times. Later years, I communicated with Christmas cards. The last time we communicated was Christmas 1981.

* * *

On the drive back, the detective urged me to call my mother. He said, "It's your decision; although, it might make things easier on everyone if you spoke to her before you left here. What do you think?"

"I don't know. I don't want to talk to them." He kept trying to convince me until I consented. Reluctantly, I used his office and made the call.

When the phone rang, Dad accepted the collect call. "Hello, Ken?"

"Uh—oh—hi Dad—let me talk to Mother."

"Okay, before I do, I want to tell you I was wrong to let my anger get out of control. Now hang on and I'll get your mother. Hey—June, Ken's on the phone."

The first thing to come to my mind, *The bastard did not even apologize for beating the shit out of me. I am going back to the same old bullshit.* Then I recognized my Mother's voice.

"Hello, Ken?"

"Hi Mother."

She started the same old routine of how much she loved me, and blah, blah, blah. I ignored her. I was convinced these were false promises. I had found people who cared about me here, and now I was being forced to leave them. The detective walked in with coffee and indicated he wanted to talk to my parents.

"Mother, I've got to go. Detective Andersen wants to talk to you. Bye." I handed the phone to the detective. As I stood in the hallway, he gave her all the details of my return trip on the train.

When he hung up, he said, "Ken, come on in here." As I entered, he indicated for me to sit down. "Okay, I've got you on the seven o'clock train. You and your police escort will have a private Pullman room. Depending on the weather, you should get into Glasgow by noon on Saturday. Until we have to leave for the train station, the lieutenant's office has a couch and you can go in there and take a nap. Can I trust you to not run off or do I need to handcuff you to a chair?"

I turned and glared at him. I walked down to the lieutenant's office and lay down. Within minutes, I was asleep. I awoke to Detective Andersen shaking me. Standing with him was a young man dressed in blue jeans, boots, and a Western shirt. Detective Andersen introduced him: "This is Officer Mason. He will be making the trip with you."

Officer Mason was smiling. "My name is Allen. I hope we can have a pleasant trip. Do you understand what I'm saying?"

As I sat up rubbing my eyes, I said, "Uh-huh. I don't want to go home, but I won't give you a hard time." It appeared I pleased both officers.

At the train station, Detective Andersen found a conductor who took us to our Pullman room. They told us as soon as the train was out of the station the dining car would be open for breakfast. Allen suggested we go to the dining car now to reserve a table before the rush.

When we arrived at the dining car, there were people already sitting and a porter showed us to a small table by a window. As the train started to leave, I looked out the window, watching Spokane pass by. Even with everyone telling me I would be safe, I was convinced otherwise.

My thoughts turned to all that had happened. *Four weeks ago, I was sleeping in the bus depot. If it hadn't been for the McKinleys, I might still be sleeping there. Besides, Linda, she was the one who cared enough to contact John. I didn't even get to thank her. Mrs. Carroll and everyone at the store, they didn't know me, yet they treated me fantastic. I can't believe I'm going back.*

As Spokane disappeared behind us, the events of the last four weeks replayed in my head. I turned away from Allen and stared out the window. I was fighting the tears as the train headed east.

Chapter 6 – The Truce

"In the attic of his childhood was an old trunk
and even though he couldn't pry it open,
the muffled sobs coming from inside
told him more than he wanted to remember."

— e9Art

We had delays on the trip back to Glasgow and it was after five pm Saturday when we arrived. Even though we had a private room and bunks, sleeping on the train was difficult. I was exhausted by the time we arrived. As we pulled into the station, I spotted Mother waiting, but I did not see my dad. When the train stopped, Allen had me stay onboard while he went to talk to Mother. They talked briefly, he returned to our room, we grabbed our bags, and we disembarked. Allen would spend the night in a motel waiting to catch a return train the next day.

When I got off, Mother came rushing over to me in tears. "Oh son—you don't know how happy I am to see you." She hugged and kissed me. "I love you. I'm so glad you're home. Things will be better, you'll see."

"I love you too," I mumbled while looking around for Dad. "Where's Dad?"

"He's waiting in the car. It is so cold and windy here; we took turns watching for the train."

They closed the train depot in Glasgow. Unless someone was to get on or off, the passenger train did not stop. You had to purchase your ticket at the bus depot. Allen was walking off in the opposite direction. I yelled, "Hey Allen—Thank you." He turned, gave me a wave, and then continued on his way.

I was feeling sorry for him. He would get a few hours sleep and then he would be back on the train heading for Spokane. This time he wouldn't be in a Pullman; it was coach class all the way. Since my parents agreed to pay the expenses for my return, I don't know why they didn't book him a Pullman on the return trip.

The wind was blowing and it was bitter cold. While I was gone, they had several inches of snow. To make things even more miserable, the wind was whipping the snow in my face. I followed Mother to the car and when Dad saw us coming, he got out of the car, opened the trunk, and quickly got back in. Not once did he say anything or even look at me. Mother was already in the front passenger seat by the time I loaded my duffle bag and shut the trunk.

Okay, that was stupid. If I want to run, my duffle bag is in the trunk. I kept trying to get myself to calm down. Yet, with the lack of a warm reception, I wanted to be anywhere but there. I stood thinking, *Yeah – welcome home, Kenny.*

I could hear Mother saying something to Dad and the tone of her voice was anything but kind. He was giving her the cold stare. I reached for the back door of the car and found it locked. I tapped on the window, but no one acknowledged me. I rapped harder a second time and still I was not acknowledged. I stepped up front and smacked hard on the windshield.

Dad looked up at me, his face turned red, and he rolled down his window. "What?"

"Would you mind unlocking the car door? Or do you want me to walk home?"

"Don't get smart with me. I'll knock your teeth – "

"William!" Mother shouted. "Now just stop it!"

Dad mumbled something inaudible as he rolled up his window. Even when it was freezing out side, the sweat began to trickle from my underarms. *What the hell am I doing here? They don't give a shit about me.*

Dad reached around and unlocked the back door. I opened it and stuck in my head. "Open the trunk for me so I can get my bag. I'll leave and you will never have to see me again."

Mother yelled, "Kenny — Please!"

"If you didn't want me here, why in the hell did you force me to come back?"

Mother continued, "Kenny — Please. Get in the car so we can go home. I promise — "

I interrupted, "Why — I haven't been here five minutes and he's already threatening me. He's NOT going to hit me again — unlock the damn trunk — I want my bag."

Dad opened his door and got out. I started backing up, getting ready to either swing at him or run. I wanted to hit him even if it meant getting the shit beat out of me. He did not move in my direction. What I observed in my dad's eyes, I had never seen before. It appeared it was painful having to look at me. Any anger was absent. There was only sadness in his eyes. "Your mother is right. Things will be different. I know I cannot take my anger out on you. It is not right. So please, get in the car, and let's go home."

It was if his eyes were begging and I didn't know what to do. *What's going on? One second he's ready to knock my head off and the next he looks like he might cry.* Perhaps it was those begging eyes, but I didn't say anything; I got into the car.

Mother said, "Thank you Kenny," and then she started crying.

Dad didn't say a word; he started the car and drove us home. I sat there in a stupor, trying to understand what had just happened. Never had I seen my dad like this. *Could he be sorry? Why didn't he apologize? What's going on?*

Once Mother recovered, she started asking questions about my trip. I answered, but my mind was elsewhere. Even with Dad's sadness, I still wasn't convinced things would change. *I had better start planning my escape. This time, I will go somewhere where they won't think to look and they won't catch me.*

* * *

Although my parents were congenial, the next few days at home were stressful. They were polite, but they never mentioned anything about the last four-plus weeks. They never inquired about my time in Spokane. In fact, we never did talk about what had happened or what we would do to prevent it from happening again. As with previous incidents through the years, they acted as if it had never happened.

I didn't understand why I was feeling guilty. *What did I do? Dad was the one who beat the crap out of me.* Mother condoned it by making excuses for him. *So why am I feeling as if it is my fault?* I couldn't understand their attitude or my feelings. The consequences were a depression that lasted weeks.

My parents had always been against my smoking. In the past, I would attempt to hide it. They weren't naïve, they were aware of my smoking. When I returned, I was bold and did not try to hide it, and subsequently they said little. I would step outside and smoke in plain view of them. It was if I was challenging them to say something. *Come on – say something about my smoking. Give me an excuse to run again.* I was being stupid, but I didn't care.

I called the McVees letting them know I was home. I got a warm reception, but then Charles said, "Why did you run? Didn't you trust us to protect you?"

"Yes, I trusted you. I didn't trust my dad." I told Charles about John and Marianne McKinley and how they took me in.

Charles said, "Promise me if the bullshit starts again, you will call me – promise."

"I promise. I'm sorry I didn't call you from Spokane. I was so scared — "

Charles interrupted, "What's important, you are safe now. By the way, if you want a job next summer, you've got one here." I thanked him and the following summer I did work for Charles again.

I also periodically drove out to visit the ranch. I loved being there and enjoyed their caring friendship. As I did with the McKinleys, I corresponded with Charles and Marlene, especially at Christmas. As with the McKinleys, I kept the correspondence going until 1981.

* * *

The following Monday, I caught the bus and returned to school. They required me to meet with the principal. I assumed someone had notified him, because he was informed I had run away, but was unaware of the details. I was feeling ashamed and when a teacher or classmate asked anything; I was evasive. It was only a couple of my closest friends whom I told the details to. I asked them to keep it confidential. In reality, no one really cared. Most of my friends treated me as if nothing had happened. We picked up where we had left off. They told me what had gone on in my absence. Life went on.

Teachers were sympathetic when it came to homework and they helped with the process of catching up. I worked hard and studied every evening and on weekends. Within six weeks, I was caught up with most of my classes. My grades were not great, but then I was never an A-student. Even when school and my social life returned to normal, my home life did not.

In the beginning, Mother went overboard attempting to compensate for what had occurred. She would cook some of my favorite meals, and she constantly asked if I was okay. It was easy to interpret it all as a façade. She had never been demonstrative to show compassion, why now? Her empathy was short-lived and soon she was back to being abrasive and manipulative.

Although I didn't understand it at the time, there was a definite change in Dad and my relationship. As normal, he showed little interest in what I did. For the most part, he ignored me. He never apologized, even though I sensed he was embarrassed. Dad would find things to do that kept him away from the house. He would also spend time working on projects in the basement or in the garage. I'm not sure exactly what precipitated the change in Dad. I always thought it was the embarrassment of the military reprimanding him. He was a proud man and a perfectionist with everything. This would have shown a flaw in his character and he would have trouble accepting it.

Dad showed his regret for what had happened in several ways. When Mother was being her normal curt self, he would speak up and defend me. "What's the big deal, let him enjoy his time in high school." At first, it was confusing. *Why was he supporting me?* I was used to the harsh reprimands. After the first couple of times, I quit paying attention to Mother; Dad wouldn't say anything or get angry with me.

The tension between my parents heightened. I would hear them argue daily. Dad still had little control over his anger. As before, he would throw or break things. What he did not do was vent his anger towards me. If annoyed or angry with me, I would see him turn red and start to explode. He would catch himself and then walk away. Mother would scold me for upsetting him and later I would hear their argument.

I found it too painful and emotionally difficult to talk to anyone. I didn't want anyone to know what had happened or what was occurring now. I now recognize I was suffering with depression. I also did not realize the long-term effect this had on my self-esteem. At this age, you didn't realize you were making it more difficult on yourself, by not confronting the problem.

* * *

I didn't think Dad conscientiously took advantage of the situation as an effort to apologize. However, during the Christmas holidays, over dinner, he said, "One of the young guys who work for me is being transferred overseas He has a nice Chevy he needs to sell. I looked at it and it looks like it is in good shape. You think you might be interested?"

"Yes. Sir." I was ecstatic thinking about having my own car. I first thought, *Is he going to finally buy me a car?* Quickly, I remembered him saying; if I wanted a car, I would have to pay for it myself. *Is he saying he will help me buy a car? Calm down; listen to what he is saying.*

I started thinking of all the things I could do with my own car. *I can go to all the school activities. I won't have to beg to use his car anymore. If he starts to threaten me again, I can get in my car and take off.* My mind went wild with endless advantages of having my own car. I hadn't been this excited in a long time.

Dad said nothing, as he seemed to enjoy my excitement. I was all but jumping out of my chair. "I will talk with this airman tomorrow and if he hasn't already sold it, I will tell him you're interested."

Dad took me the next evening to have a look. He had said a Chevy, but he did not say what year. I was thinking '54 or '55 or older. It thrilled me when I recognized it was a '57. Dad did the negotiation and we purchased it for $400, $150 less than he was asking. Since he was leaving the next week, I benefited from his desperation.

Dad handled the title and I paid the airman from my credit union account. Dad also made me an offer I didn't refuse. If, during the week, I would allow him to drive the car to work, he would pay for the insurance. I wasn't stupid — how could I pass this offer up? As it turned out, I never needed the car when he was driving it. He sold the old Buick, and the offer worked to his and my advantage.

Over the next months, when I had the opportunity, I would take the car over to the base hobby shop. Two airmen who hung out there liked my car. They convinced me to allow them to modify it. They would do the work if I paid for the parts. Again, it was a great offer I didn't pass up. By the end of the following summer, and for an investment of $250, I swapped my six-cylinder for a small block 283 V-8. I also upgraded the transmission to match. They painted the car and put in a radio. They changed the interior from cloth to vinyl, and put reversed rim wheels with moon hubcaps. It looked hot.

Mother thought it was foolish spending more money on the car, while Dad never said a word. When they completed it, he told me he was sure getting some looks. He said, "All the young airmen are all over the car. They keep asking if I want to sell it. I tell them it is my son's car. You'll have to ask him."

I had no interest in selling it; it was my prize possession. I kept the '57 Chevy until 1966.

* * *

It was in September of 1964, when I had started my senior year, that Dad received orders to go to Kinchloe AFB. "Where's Kinchloe?" I asked Mother.

"I'm not sure other than it's somewhere in Michigan." After extensively looking at our road atlas, we found it up near Sault Ste. Marie and the Canadian border.

I made a futile attempt to stay with a friend to finish high school at Glasgow. Dad never offered his opinion; however, Mother was emphatic I would move with them.

Sometime in October, we packed my parents' car and mine and headed for Michigan. As with previous moves, we moved into guest housing until our furniture arrived. The base did not have

98

any schools and they bused us to the small community of Rudyard next to the base.

Kinchloe AFB was smaller and older than the base at Glasgow, but our house was the largest base house in which we had ever lived. It was a three-bedroom split-level built against a hill. It was at the end of the street and backed up to the woods. It was a beautiful setting and I used to take walks in the woods. Within a mile from our house was a ski lift and slope the base had built. I tried several times to learn to ski, but I was never successful.

When I started at Rudyard High School, I was the new kid and I was feeling out of place. This was the first time I entered a new school alone. I don't think I was timid. One of the first individuals I met was Mary. She introduced me to her group. They made me feel welcome and helped me integrate into school activities. Within weeks, I began participating in activities at school. My group ran the refreshment stand for basketball games. The music teacher found out I played the trumpet, and he encouraged me to join the band. Again, my stupid pride refused to let go and I turned him down. It was a mistake I regretted.

As I always did, I wanted my independence and having more money would promote this goal. I was able to get a job working at the warehouse for the Base Exchange. I only worked on Saturdays; the job didn't interfere with school or its activities. It gave me plenty of spending money and gas for my car.

During my senior year, my relationship with my parents could be described as indifference. Mother attempted to restrain my independence, but Dad again came to my defense. "Let him be, it is his last year in school. Let him enjoy it." My grades in my senior year were the best through high school.

Dad continued to use my car during the week in exchange for paying the insurance. At first, it wasn't a conflict. As the year progressed, I found more needs for the car. Dad didn't protest; he used Mother's car. When Mother's complaints became intolerable, he bought himself an old pickup. When he did, I had to pay for my own insurance. In 1964, insurance wasn't expensive, especially if you were on your parents' policy, as I was.

* * *

A member of the group I hung out with was Charlie, whose mother was German. Charlie worked with me at the warehouse for the Base Exchange. As our friendship grew, many Saturday evenings after work, we would end up at Charlie's house. His dad had turned their basement into a family room with a couch, TV, pool table, and a small bar. We spent many Saturday nights playing pool, watching TV, and sneaking beer or booze from his parents' bar. If we started drinking, I would call my parents and tell them I was staying overnight. When we would continue drinking, I would end up crashing on the couch.

Both Charlie and his mother were good skiers. Several times, we spent the weekend at a ski lodge or made an excursion into Canada. Wherever she took us, we would have dinner with Charlie's mother and then go out on our own. If it hadn't been for our friendship, my senior year might not have been as memorable.

My parents never questioned the extensive time I spent over at Charlie's house or the Canadian trips. Mother was working part-time as a nurse and Dad found activities keeping him away from the house. Most likely, it pleased Mother; she didn't have to deal with me. Unless there was a task Dad needed done, he was indifferent.

That winter we received over 200 inches of snow. Most mornings, Dad had me up early shoveling the driveway for him to be able to leave for work. Even after school, I often would come home and shovel snow. Before spring, I had the snow piled to over twelve feet on each side of the driveway. When it became impossible to throw the snow higher, I had to move the piles out into the yard to make room for more snow. This is one of the reasons as an adult I have never wanted to live up north.

As graduation time approached, I began to make my plans. I had already informed my parents that once I graduated, I was leaving home. Mother's reply was, "Whatever you do, you had better do it right. Once you leave, don't even think about coming back."

Dad surprised me, "Why don't you stay here for the summer. You have a job at the warehouse; if they will give you more hours, why run off?" I thought Dad would have been the one eager for me to leave. I was wrong.

Pat and her husband had moved to Ames, Iowa, the location of Iowa State University. When they offered to fix a room for me in their basement, I agreed. I applied and the school accepted me for the fall semester. One of my plans was to ask Pat if I could come after graduation and find a job in Ames.

Before we graduated, Charlie told me he was going with his mother to Germany. She insisted Charlie and his younger sister go with her for the summer. With Charlie leaving, there was no way was I going to stay at home for the summer. I was determined to find work somewhere that took me away from home. Farmers in the area hired high school boys in the summer. Unlike working at the McVee's ranch where you stayed on the ranch, you had to commute daily to the farms.

Mackinaw Island, a resort area about fifty miles from Kinchloe, hired college and high school kids for the summer season. Mackinaw Island didn't allow motorized vehicles on the island. It was exclusively bicycles and horse-pulled carriages. Before graduation, I went to Mackinaw Island and put in my application at several places. With my experience with horses at the McVee ranch, they hired me for the Grand Hotel working at their stable. It was not a great job, but it would keep me away from home for the summer.

For my senior prom, Charlie and I double-dated. Charlie and I both dumped our dates after the prom dance and went with several other boys to the woods to drink. I woke up the next morning, again on the couch at Charlie's house.

Graduation was bittersweet. I was sad because Charlie was leaving. In fact, it was the last time I was with Charlie. Charlie was the one who should have gone on to college, yet he didn't. Before the year ended, they drafted him into the Army and several months later they sent him to Vietnam. I lost track of Charlie when he left the military. Years later, with a search on the Internet, I found out Charlie had lived in California and died when he was thirty-five.

With graduation, I became apprehensive. I was eager to leave home, yet the uncertainty of being on my own was scary. I recalled the period when I ran away from home, how lonely I was. Even when I wanted to leave, being on my own was frightening. I worried if I would feel the same way. As it turned out, I worried for nothing.

I had a great summer working on Mackinaw Island. During the summer, I had opportunities to return home, yet I didn't. When I checked in at the Grand Hotel the first morning, they told me one of the carriage drivers resigned and they offered me the job. I spent the summer driving a carriage for the Grand Hotel. The Grand Hotel had dorms over the stables for the summer help. I made friends and when we weren't working, there was always a group ready to have some fun.

* * *

At the end of the summer, I left just enough time to return home, pack my things, and drive to Iowa. School was to start the next week. I found the house in an uproar. Dad had gotten orders for Korea. Mother was furious. She wanted him to retire and for them to move to Texas. She threatened to divorce him if he accepted the assignment to Korea.

I can only speculate, but Dad wasn't opposed to the assignment and their separation for eighteen months. He had close to thirty years in the Air Force and could have retired; yet, he didn't. I remember I asked him why he stayed married to my mother. He didn't get mad when I asked. I witnessed the same sadness in his eyes I had seen eighteen months earlier. He sighed and stated, "I take my marriage vows seriously. Your mother can be a pain in the ass, but I still would rather be with her than without her. I don't know, maybe I still love her."

After I left for school, two months later, Dad left for Korea. Before he left, Mother moved to Dallas and returned full-time to her nursing profession. Mother never did follow through with her threat. The few letters I received from Dad while he was in Korea, he sounded lonely, but enjoyed the break from Mother.

The day I left our home at Kinchloe AFB, I was so excited and apprehensive, if that makes sense. It excited me that the day had finally come when I was leaving home and would be on my own. I didn't have to worry about pleasing my Dad or listening to Mother's belittling remarks. I was on my own and could do whatever I wanted. On the other hand, I was going into the adult world where I was responsible for my own subsistence.

Would I be able to find a job in Ames? Was college going to be as difficult as I had been told? My sister and I hadn't lived together since she got married. She now had a little boy. *Would we get along now?*

With my '57 Chevy loaded with all my possessions, I headed south towards Iowa. The music was blaring from the radio and the wind was blowing through the open windows. At that moment, I was feeling invincible and happier than I had ever been. Nothing was going to break my spirit. One of my favorite songs came on the radio. I turned the volume up and sang along.

Satisfaction

"I can't get no satisfaction, I can't get no satisfaction

'Cause I try and I try and I try and I try

I can't get no, I can't get no

When I'm drivin' in my car, and the man comes on the radio

He's tellin' me more and more about some useless information

Supposed to fire my imagination

I can't get no, oh, no, no, no, hey, hey, hey

That's what I say

I can't get no satisfaction, I can't get no satisfaction

'Cause I try and I try and I try and I try

I can't get no, I can't get no...satisfaction"

Music and lyrics by Mick Jagger and Keith Richards of the Rolling Stones

Conclusion, But Not The End

"You are allowed to terminate your relationship
with toxic family members.
You are allowed to walk away from people who hurt you.
You are allowed to be angry and selfish...
You don't owe anyone an explanation for taking care of YOU."
— Unknown Author

My story doesn't end with leaving home and heading to college. Far from it, but we will leave those events for another time. What did end was the physical abuse I suffered growing up. What did not end was the mental and controlling abuse from my parents. I didn't understand then and I don't understand today how I allowed it to continue.

In retrospect, I see myself like women who tolerate their abusive spouses. When Mother would remind me of all the things they did for me as a child, I would feel guilty. When Mother would tell me I was worthless and I would never amount to anything, I recognized she was wrong. Yet, I continued the debilitating behavior of trying to please her and my dad. If they would accept me, as who I am, I could finally be happy. That didn't happen. Yet like a puppy dog someone kicked, I came back, hoping to find acceptance and especially love.

* * *

For more years than I want to admit, I had the feeling of obligation to my parents. Holidays and special occasions, I would go to their home. Even when I lived three hundred miles away, I would take time off to make sure I attended family functions. To not attend showed disrespect and being unappreciative for what they had done for me as my parents. I had succumbed to Mother's brainwashing and continued to allow her to manipulate me. I would submit to the demands rather than deal with the consequences.

As my dad aged, the fiery anger was not as pronounced. He became more tolerant and even showed interest in me. When I was in the military, I saw him looking at me with pride. Although just as when I was young, he never communicated his feelings. As I matured, I understood my dad more. I still lived with the unrealistic expectations that someday he would show me his love.

Dad also surrendered to Mother's demands. Once he retired from the military, he told me it was easier to give in to her than to fight her. He often said, "What difference does it make, just let her have her way. When you do, you don't have to listen to her complain."

* * *

What is prevalent with many abuse survivors is low self-esteem, little self-confidence, guilt, and periods of debilitating depression. I suffered from them all. I did not understand what was wrong with me when I would quit rather than confront life's challenges. I struggled to complete college. When career opportunities availed themselves, I shunned them. I was always uncomfortable with personal relationships. My peers moved forward while I sat in the shadows.

Even when I pushed myself to the physical and mental limits and succeeded in becoming a member of the Air Force's Special Forces Pararescue Team (PJs), I had no self-pride. When I put my life at risk along side my fellow PJs, I thought I was inferior to them. When I received a medal for my valor in Vietnam, I did not appreciate the recognition. For years, I hid the fact that I had served in the military with honors. Now as a decorated Vietnam Veteran, I stand with pride.

I'm not the first person to describe depression as that inner person who takes control and thrusts us into a period of ineptness. That person is no longer a stranger when he visits me and I know there is no satisfying his destructive disposition. Often my stranger's visits come without warning and he stays beyond his welcome. While he visits, I become withdrawn or overly needy. My stranger brings blame for the mistakes I have made in my life. When he leaves, I'm left with his two companions, guilt and defeat.

When I was young, I did not know what depression was and that I was suffering from it. No one explained that the overwhelming feelings of shame and confusion were symptoms of depression. What I do remember is the desire for acceptance and happiness. Finding it was an insurmountable endeavor.

I was my worst critic. Anything I did required perfection. When it wasn't accomplished, I had feelings of inadequacy. In hindsight, pleasing myself was as impossible as pleasing my dad. This is the reason why I struggled for years with low self-esteem and little self-confidence.

When it came to relationships, it was no wonder I struggled. If I found someone willing to show me affection, I pushed them away or became dependent. I didn't know how to share intimacy. I always looked to the other person to bring happiness into my life. I had no concept of self-happiness.

When I married at age twenty, I didn't love my wife. She was my closest friend and I enjoyed her companionship. I also recognized that she was a beautiful woman and other men wanted to date her. It was weeks before we married I recognized she was in love with me. A year after we married, it came to me that I indeed loved her. I had from the beginning, but didn't understand those emotions.

When I was in my thirties, I had a horrible and traumatic episode. As a result, I went into a clinical depression and I was even hospitalized. I became non-functional and, for a period, suicidal. I spent years in and out of extensive psychological therapy to overcome severe periods of anxiety and depression. As when I was young, some type of instinct helped me survive and I became stronger.

My last therapist helped me break through the psychological barriers. She helped me understand that the link between my guilt, low self-esteem, and depression were the years of child abuse. She helped me deal with the self-anger and the suppressed anger towards my parents. She helped me understand that happiness came from within. You didn't need to please others to be happy. She also helped me understand my depression, and the techniques to keep it in check. She helped me attain a new life of security and happiness I didn't know was achievable.

Even with all the psychological problems I experienced, I did attain an accounting degree and passed my CPA exams. I had a successful career in public and governmental accounting.

I was fortunate that I found the love of my life and we have been together over thirty-three years. I found that I could receive and give love without feeling manipulated or guilty. I don't need anyone else to be happy, yet it's enhanced when it is shared with that special person in your life.

* * *

Friends will tell you I still live in a world with unrealistic expectations. I don't want to believe people are innately evil. In my own defense, I refuse to believe hatred controls our world. There has to be decency intermingled with the hostility. Good has to win over evil.

I believe there are underlying circumstances that cause parents to abuse their children. I don't accept that my parents were inherently malicious. There were reasons behind the years of child abuse. There were reasons why the same hostility I experienced as a child continued when I was an adult.

Obviously, Dad had an anger problem and was unable or unwilling to do anything about it. The anger was a character flaw and was the underlying reason why he had problems with self-confidence. He compensated his lack of confidence with being a perfectionist and an overachiever. His perfectionism carried over to him demanding I meet the same standards. When I didn't, the results were harsh discipline. Yet, it doesn't justify the beatings, especially the ones where he used his fist.

I have concluded Mother never agreed to, yet went along with, the adoption. From the beginning, she resented having to raise me. When I came with emotional baggage, it further frustrated her. This left her with the responsibility of dealing with me. Mother had no empathy for weak individuals. She had no problem using people to get what she wanted.

I conclude the abuse was initiated from their failure to be honest with each other. Neither of them had the initiative to take the steps to end their inexcusable behavior. Their harboring of guilt and anger was the foundation for my abuse as a child and their bitterness towards me as an adult. I acknowledge this is oversimplified. Right or wrong, this is my explanation.

* * *

It took years, but I finally conquered the obsession of trying to please my parents. As I overcame the debilitating behavior, we became estranged. The estrangement did not happen overnight. The more I didn't succumb to Mother's control and Dad's indifference, the more resentment there was between us. With the resentment came more estrangement.

All the years we did not speak, I did not give up on my fantasy of reconciliation. I never missed a birthday, anniversary, Christmas, Mother's and Father's Day without sending a card. I sent gifts for special occasions (e.g. Fiftieth Anniversary). When someone told me Mother would take my cards or gifts and throw them in the trash unopened, I stopped. Yet, I never stopped hoping someday something would happen to change their mind.

Even when estranged, I kept track of them. I would search the Dallas County Texas Tax Assessor's website to verify their home was still in their name. I would query the local newspapers for their obituaries. In 2000, I checked the Tax Assessor's website; I found the taxes were unpaid, yet the house was still in my parents' name.

On crosschecking, I found the filing of the probate of Dad's will. He had died in July of 1997 and Pat had waited until 2000 to file the probate. In further checking, I found Mother had preceded him in death in February of the same year. Both of them resided in a nursing facility until their death.

My parents were dead for over three years and no one, including Pat, had the decency to notify me. How could people be so insensitive as not notify a member of the immediate family of a death? It was not a surprise when I read the will. There was a paragraph dedicated to ensure I inherited nothing from my parents' estates.

* * *

Since my retirement several years ago, I've fought cancer twice. My first was bladder cancer and later Non-Hodgkin's Lymphoma. While going through chemotherapy and its effects, I was often housebound. As a distraction, I wrote my life story.

While ill from the side effects of the chemotherapy, days melted into weeks and months as I immersed myself in my writing. I did not understand it at the time, but the act of writing about those years was emotionally healing.

I brought to the forefront feelings I had harbored and refused to acknowledge. I had forgotten many of the horrors. I began to overcome the emotional scars from the years of child abuse. Admitting to these character weaknesses was the first step to recovery. Realizing my parents didn't need to be controlling my life was the next. By writing, I put those emotions in their proper perspective. The final key was the restoration of my faith in God.

A good friend advised me that if I wanted to overcome the anger I had towards my parents, I should pray for them. I began to pray for God to forgive them. Later, I read that for God to forgive those who have hurt us, we must first forgive them ourselves.

One day I was fighting a depression and I went to one of my favorite places to meditate. While I prayed, the words of my friend came to me. I prayed for God to give me the strength to finally forgive my parents. As I prayed, the emotions came pouring out. I found myself sobbing and telling my parents I was sorry for my anger and I forgave them.

When I recovered, it was a new day and the sun was brighter. I had found the clear glass where the prism of color, sunshine, and happiness shone in. Those experiences from the past were not forgotten; they became insignificant. I grasped the beauty of my life and not the negativity of the anger. I was able to forgive my parents and I acknowledged God could now give them peaceful repose.

All the hurt and anger was no longer controlling. I recognized I didn't need their love and acceptance to attain true happiness. I had attained it already. I was finally at peace with my parents. What was more significant, I was at peace with myself.

"I no longer need to maintain abusive relationships. As I continue to grow and heal, I attract those people who love me for who I am. I have no need to hide myself. I have no need to deny my feelings, or to disguise my thoughts and beliefs. I will no longer tolerate people who put me down, manipulate me, or humiliate me. I am surrounding myself with people who are consistently loving and respectful."

— A. Moho